To my brother Jon, JP, who reintroduced me to the band:

Love you live!

TABLE OF CONTENTS

FORWARD

For 30 years, fans of the greatest rock and roll band in the world would count on the radio, various magazines, an occasional appearance on a TV show, and that very rare live concert where they would not only get to experience the Rolling Stones live, but also meet other fans who shared their love for the band. However, once the show was over, most returned to their normal lives, having no way to really communicate with the fans they met.

In the mid-1990s, the internet found its way to rock and roll. From a few list groups, to the AOL Rolling Stones chat and Undercover and Gasland, to the development of huge Stones message boards like SHIDOOBEE, IORR, and Rocks Off, suddenly there sprang up communities of people from all over the world who were able to not only share their devotion to the Stones, but also, now get together in large groups to celebrate the music of the band. Whether it be a party before or after a concert, or an annual gathering of Stones fans in Wildwood N.J., people now were able to converse with others who had the same devotion they had. Life long friendships and marriages developed, all because of the new communication form and the people that kept these sites exciting.

Andee brings all these aspects together in a book that for the first time shows people who, in the past, might be very private, and now, would drop everything to travel around the world to see the Stones and party with some of their greatest fans. Put on your favorite Stones album, turn it up loud, and enjoy the experiences of this passionate group.

Doug Potash
www.shidoobee.com

1

INTRODUCTION:

"START ME UP: THE ROLLING STONES FAN PROJECT"

"That's the soundtrack of my life...I hear at least one Stones song a day." (Chicago_Dave)

When my parents saw The Rolling Stones on TV back in the fall of 1964, they were speechless. I had rarely, if ever, known them without words. Certainly The Beatles did not have that effect on them seven months earlier. I knew something was up. They sat quietly through the band's rendition of Chuck Berry's rock tune *Around and Around*. When the ballad *Time is on Our Side* started later in the show, they really didn't know what to make of the band with their long hair and mismatched clothes. The camera panned in on Mick, singing seductively to the screaming girls. He was no Paul, the boyishly cute Beatle.

A fan since watching the band on the Ed Sullivan show at home when I was in high school, I quickly adopted The Rolling Stones into my musical library of the times. I didn't follow them too closely for a while when life events intervened, not going to any of the live shows until much later on. My two younger siblings and I each bought *Sticky Fingers* shortly after its release. My sister showed my brother and me how the real hardware on the album cover unzipped the black jeans to uncover the white briefs underneath when we reunited for Thanksgiving. As if we didn't know. We all laughed, in sibling unity.

3

I lost track of the band after that, picking up on them again with the *Some Girls* album of 1978. I didn't get my hands on that until almost two years after it came out, astonished by how really good it was. In the dark about the feud between Mick and Keith that almost destroyed the band, I missed that they weren't out on tour for most of the 80's, between 1982 until 1989, with the *Steel Wheels* tour and album. I learned later that Ronnie Wood, the newest member of the core band brought them back together by suggesting one make a call, that the other would welcome. Looking back to my record collection, in LP format, I had more Stones than any other artists except the Beatles and Bob Dylan. Most of the fans I've talked to have owned far more complete collections than mine, especially if exposed to their music early in their lives. Nonetheless, my personal introduction to the Stones and their music happened in 1964, on television.

For me, the primal story of the sixties, also captured retrospectively in tales preserved on film by Philippe Puicouyoul in his visual ode to Stones fans *Vers l'Olympe* (2008), is from the time my parents threw me out of the house. This was a classic case of a generation gap that was widening by the day. The only cigarette smoker in the family, I snuck puffs outside and had recently been introduced to toking of another kind. I had started going out with men, most not introduced to the family. I worked part-time while going to school full-time. That's what I signed up for anyway.

Living in my two-room apartment with a girl from an affluent family I didn't know before she took me in, one fall morning, I heard "Get Off Of My Cloud," pounding through the ceiling over my bed. The lyrics seemed particularly apt that day: "Two's a crowd on my cloud!" As someone who had always liked people, not yet fond of spending time alone, I found company in Mick's voice calling out "Hey, you!" and a strange solace in the driving sound of the guitars and drums. This was our music, our very own, as we tried and tried to get some "satisfaction" in our changing world. My younger brother recalls me talking about this

4

time period, likening himself to the Fred Savage character "Kevin Arnold", identifying me with the older hippie sister in the show *The Wonder Years*.

Marriage at twenty-one to a computer programmer partially overshadowed my passion for the Stones. He was a fan of classical music, with an occasional folk artist like Odetta or Judy Collins in the mix. I certainly didn't conceive of joining the large coliseum audiences in Milwaukee, Wisconsin or Cleveland, Ohio, places we lived during the early phases of knowing each other. We went to a "Be-in" before we got married, and shortly after that, he converted to selected rock songs, liking "White Rabbit" because of its lyrics about chess-playing. The largest audience my then hubby and I were in was for Arlo Guthrie at the Cleveland Agora, to hear "Alice's Restaurant" a few years after its release. When I finally finished college and started graduate school in sociology, the Stones drifted further from the center of my consciousness. After the divorce and a reintroduction to *Sticky Fingers* by a musically inclined grad student, I greatly admired "Can't You Hear Me Knocking," a song I treasure to this day. I hadn't met anyone else who talked about Stones concerts within my academic circles, and a few years after that, the band stopped touring, as it turned out, for seven years.

Not until my brother took me to the *Live at the Max* film (1992) after the *Steel Wheels* tour that started in '89 did I come to see how publicly underrated the group was at the time, how underestimated, what with all the jokes in the media about their age that seem to have been around forever. Early on, even their front man said in 1966 that he couldn't picture himself rock and rolling at age fifty, onstage singing *Satisfaction*. In the archival interview footage from 1964 shown in Scorsese's *Shine a Light*, Mick expressed uncertainty about the band lasting more than a couple of years after they first started performing, if something new came along. To say I was blown away by the filmed show is an understatement. When the next tour came along in 1994, *Voodoo*

Lounge, a new friend took me to three different concerts in two states. That was a concept previously foreign to me, traveling to shows outside of my local area. Since then I saw at least a couple of shows on every tour, more in number each time they toured. Leaving the U.S. to visit London in the Stones home country I saw two of the three concerts that ended the 2005-2007 tour, *A Bigger Bang*. Finally I was lucky to go to five shows on *50 and Counting* between late 2012 and summer 2013. Passport issues in 2014 trashed my plans for the pit at the Waldbühne in Berlin for *14 on Fire*.

Before *A Bigger Bang* kicked off, in my rekindled Stones passion, I started exploring the online fan groups, including rollingstones.com, Shidoobee, It's Only Rock 'n Roll (IORR), Rocks Off (RO), and the electronic mailing list called Undercover (UC). I post online under the nicknames "andee" or "angee." After a year or so of reading and posting as a fan, I had the idea that I could look at the members and their online communities from an internet researcher's standpoint. A sociologist by training, I had studied the areas of families, organizations, social movements and communities in graduate school. In the mid-1990s, I began to examine how couples met online to form relationships that migrated offline, resulting in an academic book called *Double Click* (Hampton Press, 2005.) For the fan project, I asked Shidoobee founder Stonesdoug if he thought I could study his group Shidoobee and he agreed, setting up a topic within his online discussion community for me to ask questions of members. Later on, for academic papers, I decided to compare fan groups to see how their cultures and technologies might make a difference to the fans who belonged. Although Shidoobee was still my center of focus, I communicated with leaders of other groups. Gazza of Rocks Off offered complete cooperation, and Bjornulf of IORR said I could contact his group's members, as did Steve Portigal for his private email list, Undercover. With the exception of Undercover, groups discussed here are public sites, accessible by anyone with a connection to the internet. My university cleared the research for scholarly publications according to their institutional review board's guidelines. This book is more personal, a journalistic account, nonfiction for a general audience of fans of rock and roll.

I chose to interview individual fans, selecting them for their active participation and for variety of ages and locations, and length of time in the group. Most people I asked accepted, even when I said that I wanted about an hour of their time. Not everyone who consented to an interview was able to follow up, a few citing work obligations as barriers to participation. Some gave me suggestions of other fans I might contact who would help the project. One hundred and three people completed interviews with me, discussing their personal histories with the music, their concert attendance with highlights of activities before and during shows. They told me their favorite person within the band, and about any band members they've met. They shared information of types of band-related artifacts they own, and apparel they've collected, not discussed here, but used in an academic article. Fans also told me how they found out about internet groups, how they selected their avatars and user IDs, and how these online communities have contributed to their fandom. I am continually struck by how much enthusiasm, how much passion the fans demonstrate for their band, feelings that mirror my own. Listening to the band's music over the years creates those emotions. In performance, the intensity of joy expressed by each audience member circles back to further inspire the band onstage.

The 103 interviews usually lasted about an hour to ninety minutes over the phone, ranging from forty minutes to almost ten hours. Many of the interviews were more like conversations, with space for back and forth talk, and the semi-structured set of questions left room for additions or adjustments for the special circumstances of various fans. A few were done in person, in chat, or through email rather than by phone or by Skype over the internet. Some people responded to requests for follow-up information in writing. The final pool of people contributing to this book represented several countries, indeed, continents. Three-quarters of interviewed fans came from within the U.S., a little over half from the eastern or southeastern U.S., with the remainder split between states in the Midwest and the West. About a quarter came from elsewhere: there were three fans from Canada, including the provinces of Quebec, Ontario, and British Columbia, six from the United Kingdom with one of those from Northern Ireland, eight from the other European countries of France, Germany, the Netherlands and Sweden, and two from the Australia/Oceana continent. Four took place with fans living in Latin American, including Mexico, Brazil, the Dominican Republic and Puerto Rico, and one with a fan from Japan. Males outnumbered females, reflecting the preponderance of men at some of the online sites, with thirty-two female fans (31%) interviewed vs. seventy-one males (69%). At the time of their interviews, their ages ranged from early twenties to mid-sixties (21 to 65), with most in their forties and fifties.

Seeking a roughly representative group of active members, I went from the discussion boards to email or private messaging to ask individuals if they would agree to be interviewed by phone. Most said yes, and most all of those completed phone interviews, or more rarely, in-person talks, or written answers in chat or by email. Along with a variety of ages and of countries of origin whenever possible, I sought people from Shidoobee, my initial focus, and then also from other online communities. Because many IORR members do not reveal their emails and there is no private messaging system there, I selected people I had met in person, those I knew from reading their posts online who listed their email addresses, or people who were referred to me from other members. With Rocks Off, I contacted people from other groups who also posted there, whereas with Undercover, a private list, I asked members who I thought could and would contribute ideas and information to the project, after the leader gave his assent for contact. In the end, two-thirds of the interviewed fans come primarily from Shidoobee (66%), although they may read and post on other groups. The rest are split mainly between IORR (17%) and Undercover (10%).

Rocks Off has the allegiance of a few fans in this project (3%), and a similar number of fans run other boards online (4%).

At no point did I attempt to draw a "random" sample from memberships lists for two reasons: first, the lists of all of those in the overall populations were not readily available to me, and, more importantly, the vast majority of the members who had ever signed up for any of the sites either dropped out quite quickly or posted so rarely, even if present, they qualified as "lurkers" rather than active members. The large non-response rate from such an attempt would have countered any effort at random representation. The people who agreed to talk to me have graciously consented to give their time, knowledge, experience and wisdom, and they are the heart of this book. The fans who completed full interviews plus fan "informants" who gave me information on specific topics are listed in the acknowledgments at the end, usually under their usernames, their online nicknames. Some have requested that I call them by their real names or other identifiers such as made-up nicknames or just "anonymous."

Fan communities are introduced with their members in the first chapter, and reappear later on, when members discuss how the online spaces affect their fan activities offline, and then also when people detail their concert experiences. Almost all fans have a preference for one or at most two communities or online discussion boards. My first home community is Shidoobee where I started under "andee," my nickname in everyday life, along with IORR (as "angee") where I go everyday, with frequent reading of the Undercover list in digest form, and mainly browsing and lurking at RO. I check the official site rollingstones.com for tickets and merchandise. Through concerts mainly in the Midwest, the New York/New Jersey area, and in Las Vegas in the U.S., in London, and at fan-organized events in the U.S. and in Europe, I have met in person over half the individuals interviewed, including community leaders Stonesdoug (Doug Potash) of Shidoobee, and Gazza (Gary Galbraith) of RO, Mickijaggeroo (Vilhelm) of Nordic Stones

Vikings, Calista Wissing from 40 Licks Fan Club of Holland, and Blue Lena (Tamara Guo) who runs The Keith Shrine. I also recently met Bjornulf Vik, head of IORR, in Newark, New Jersey.

The following chapters begin with a view of how the fans initially came to hear and like the music of The Rolling Stones and a brief look at the different communities they join online. The next chapter addresses the origins of The Stones within the countercultural trends of the 1960s, and their place alongside two other bands that started then. It's meant as a general background, a cultural analysis, the only chapter not primarily based on fan interviews. How fans name themselves on the internet, often choosing a username associated with a favorite Rolling Stone, song or album is the next chapter topic, and after that comes a chapter showing how the online world affects the ticket-buying and concert-going practices of fans.

The book continues with two chapters about going to shows, the first centering around issues for the band and their audiences during the early days of touring in the 60s through selected shows on *A Bigger Band* (*ABB*), ending in 2007. Fans at special shows or events during *Licks* and *ABB* talk about getting access to shows, traveling, and notable experiences pre-show, while hearing the music, and after. During the *50 and Counting* tour covered next, the band instituted the feature of the pit, a standing area in front of the stage. While ticket prices skyrocketed for this space, some fans decided to go for it, especially after seeing photos of how close they could be to the stage. Finally, fans that have met the band or their back-up group share their stories of how that happened in the last numbered chapter. Included here too are significant interactions between fans in the audience and band members onstage. Fans generously provided pictures of themselves with band members or back up musicians contained in a special photograph section right before this chapter. The conclusion is a coda, an epilogue, questioning possibilities for the future of the fans and the band, as Ronnie, the last of the core members and the youngest, heads toward his seventieth birthday in 2017, joining the other three.

To all the fans who helped me directly through the interviews, the online questionnaire, and in private messaging and email on select subjects, and to those who participate in the fan boards, I thank you so much. To you and everyone else who loves The Rolling Stones, rock and roll, or just good music, and to anyone who is curious about fans, I hope you enjoy the read.

CHAPTER ONE:

"CONNECTION: FINDING THE MUSIC OF THE ROLLING STONES AND JOINING FAN GROUPS"

"They just had this sound...I can't describe it...but it just grabbed you like nothing I had ever heard." (astearsgoby)

When was your first Rolling Stones concert? Where did you first see them? These questions are common in fan-to-fan talk. Another one is how old were you when you first heard the Stones? People on the fan boards compare their concert experiences to other shows during a tour, and to shows they heard ten, twenty, thirty years ago and even further back. After all, the Stones are all in or near their 70s now, so some fans are as old as they are. Most of the post-World War II generation in the States, the oldest of the Boomers, first set eyes on them with their Ed Sullivan appearance on October 1964, after their first American tour earlier that year.

Fans in England and elsewhere in the UK saw them sooner, from 1962 in London, the year Charlie Watts met the others, and then in January, 1963 officially joined the band to cap off the original core group of Mick Jagger, Keith Richards, Brian Jones, Ian Stewart, and Bill Wyman. Brian gave them their name, from the title of a Muddy Waters 1950 song, "Rollin' Stone," a name also snagged by Jann Wenner for his rock magazine *Rolling Stone* later on, in 1967. During the same decade, (1965) Bob Dylan wrote his the anthem "Like a Rolling Stone," a tune covered by many, including Hendrix, and even the Stones.

Andrea Baker

Listening for the First Time: The Songs, and the Recordings

When the Stones music started playing on the radio, it hit the listener's ears with a jolt. For those not around during the time, the impact is difficult to describe. Outside of recorded music, radio was the only media outlet for rock and roll, and indeed, any music at all in the U.S., other than an isolated hit or two on a television variety show such as Ed Sullivan or Dean Martin. American Bandstand from 1956 featured rock and pop groups but neither The Rolling Stones nor The Beatles ever appeared there. They did make it onto the British TV show *Thank Your Lucky Stars* in 1963 to play their first hit song "Come On."

After their first album, and few more popular singles came out in the UK and the States, they wrote what is perceived as their signature song, "Satisfaction." When they released "Satisfaction" in the summer of '65, youthful listeners reveled in the driving beat, related to the alienation of the anti-commercial, out of the ordinary lyrics like "and a man comes on the radio and tells you how white your shirts can be," and not the least, loved the explicitly sexual connotation of the title and the chant "I can't get no, I can't get no" in the refrain. Puppy love and holding hands had nothing on this stuff, more related to 1950s blues songs about hoochie coochie men who got their mojos working, as well as the emerging movement of hard-hitting rock and roll, increasingly led by the Brits.

Often older brothers or sisters had turned the Stones fans here onto the music through pointing it out on the radio or playing their records for them. If no relatives were around, the fans discovered the music on their own. The names of the first songs they listened to stood out in people's minds, or the albums such as "High Tide and Green Grass," an early compilation of hits in 1966, or they remembered simply the sound. The first song to come out on vinyl was that cover version of Chuck Berry's "Come On," and one very young fan "had never heard anything like it." The tune "shook" her "8-year-old tail-feather.". Another fan says the Stones' version of Willie Dixon's "Little Red Rooster" was one of the songs that first "got me hooked." Quite a few agree that whatever tune they recall first, they were hooked ever after on the music. One of those fans, Shidoobee member TinaJagger, went to the library to take out the *Hot Rocks* album, after hearing "Under My Thumb." Her ten-year-old ears had not before taken in sounds "so different and funky."

One man liked a song he heard in 1964, "It's All Over Now," and then some time later with "The Last Time," he knew he had to "buy an album and hear more." For long-lasting pleasure, he notes, "I still enjoy both songs very much today," while Thru and Thru recalls her lasting appreciation of a 1964 cover tune, "You Better Move On." A Japanese fan in Shidoobee, Far East Bam says that his initial favorites "Tell Me" and "Satisfaction" are "songs that have not parted from my ears."

Expectedly, older fans usually mentioned songs they first heard and remembered that came out early on, whereas the youngest fans referred to trigger songs as recent as "Love is Strong" from the 1990's. Fans differ in the age of exposure from very young, eight years old or even younger to well into their twenties. Younger fans have a larger catalogue of songs to hear available in various media. In his mid-forties, EG Jim reports, half jokingly, that by the time he was three he was already a Stones fan. A family photo captured him "jamming in his playpen" to "Paint It Black," according to his father. His older brother had received the album *Hot Rocks* as a gift and "was going nuts" playing "the crap out of it the whole summer" when EG was just 11 or 12:

> On side 4 was "Midnight Rambler," you know what I mean, your DNA is in there--something grabs ya. It was the beginning of my craziness that's affected almost everything in my life. When I'm down and out, it always cheers you up.

A theme especially enunciated by women is the sexual thrill they get from the band through the music they experienced at first. When watching Mick and the other boys on TV in the sixties with my parents, I felt something different going on from the everyday, an ominous undertone in the sound, yet, with a hint of sarcasm. The look in the front man's eyes and his message seemed meant just for me. My mom and dad sat in silence, a relatively rare occurrence at home, not quite knowing what to think. I found out that later that my little brother, eight at the time, knew the Stones, and especially Mick, were all "about sex," even though he hardly understood what that was.

Fans pointed to specific songs that stuck with them at the time of their introduction to the music. Struck by "She's So Cold," a cut from the 1980 album *Emotional Rescue,* a female fan described its clear impact on her impending adolescence: "I was just hitting puberty and my hormones got the best of me when I heard Mick singing. s-e-x-y!!!!!!!!" She continued:

> *...his voice...ah! I used to lay with my head on the huge speaker and just melt (and shiver.) Also, used to crank "You're SO Vain" just to hear his yummy vocals. Now I'm more mature (a little) and appreciate the music so much more. The sexiness of Mick is just the icing on a huge delicious Stones cake.*

More than one male fan appreciated "Honky Tonk Women." Blindmellon mentioned how "the intro and the provocative lyrics" attracted his attention, with the beginning lines telling of a man in Memphis meeting a tipsy woman who attempted to turn a trick on him. He found the protagonist in the song fascinating. One of the youngest fans is a Keith follower or "Keith babe" as the female fans call themselves in contrast to the "Mick chick" above. She cites "You Better Move On," a cover tune written by Arthur Alexander because it has stayed in her mind, and she "loves Keith" in the video clip of it from the 60s, where he is "so defiantly and offhandedly sexy!"

You Get What You Need

Jaggerlover writes about her early infatuation, comparing it to her later years, beginning with "Let's Spend the Night Together."

Oh My God...that was sooooo naughty way back in the early 60's and I was "underage"...just the thought of Mick singing that had me sweating back then....

Now when he sings it, it's still the same...only I think it's menopause now that has me sweating :rollin :rollin :rollin only kidding....I still react to him the same way today.

Within the youngest fan group, a confirmed Keith babe had not yet turned four years old when she listened to "Love is Strong," the first Stones song she remembers. She saw the music video and reacted strongly to Keith with "his rolled up sleeves, bare arms and dramatic arm movements." She didn't understand some of the lyrics but was afraid to think more about them for fear her mother would make her stop listening to the band.

On the more general type of excitement the music created in its listeners, the words and notes calling them to action, a fan described her Mick Jagger-wannabe boyfriend who turned up the Stones to full volume on his car radio when "19th Nervous Breakdown" came on:

He'd fly down the freeway blasting Stones Hymns. He'd slam on the brakes when Mick sang, "You'd better STOP, look around..." and then accelerate to "Here it comes, here it comes...

She added that it "scared the shit outta me half the time!" adding, in mock terror "eek, lol."

One woman's father introduced her to the Stones, although she "took off with them...without his help." The last four songs of *Flashpoint* helped her in "understanding the excitement they can produce with their music." "Jumping Jack Flash" was the "key "to her loving the Stones

17

and she still really likes "Brown Sugar," while preferring to hear it live today. Another dad took his daughter to a record store in Detroit to buy the 45rpm version of "Satisfaction," the single. She remembers

how the evening air smelled and the excitement I felt driving alongside my dad to get the record that made me fall madly in love with the Stones! All the memories of that evening come flooding back to me whenever I hear it.

Also riveted by "Jumping Jack Flash," a Toronto man recalls hearing it "one day on the radio" when he was just a kid. For days afterwards, he was singing, "but it's alriiiiiiiight now, it fact it's a gas." Mackie remembers when he was eight in 1967 and "Ruby Tuesday" played on the radio. While he had heard "Satisfaction" and "Get Off of My Cloud" before, he "literally couldn't get the that chorus out of his mind for a week." A female fan still gets goose bumps whenever she hears "Under My Thumb," a song that "locked" her "pre-teen heart up." Living in Mexico, another pre-teen recalls his mom playing "The Last Time." He enjoyed it too, repeating the words over and over at age 10 or 12, even though he didn't know English at that time.

A brother nine years older turned his little brother onto the band when he bought the single "Come On" and spun the record for him. An older sibling played the 1966 album *High Tide and Green Grass* for her younger sister, when she had not yet heard the music. The two sisters listened over and over, and "danced their little hearts out." Two females, not sisters, but best friends inspired by the Stones music, choreographed a special routine to accompany the song "Time Is on My Side" and "performed it" for their families.

Blue Lena's history with Keith and the rest of the band begins early on. At the age of eight she remembers liking the songs "Brown Sugar" and "Ruby Tuesday." Her first glimpse of the band performing was on "Don Kirshner's Rock Concert" and then later on MTV. 3DTeafoe (Daniel) saw the Stones on the Mike Douglas show in 1964 before he had even heard of them, playing "Not Fade Away," saying, "I've been hooked ever since." Very young at "seven or eight, like 3DTeafoe, Asteargoby was "hooked immediately" by "It's All Over Now," "Satisfaction," and then "As Tears Go By," his namesake song. As the band introduced each song, his "passion grew." He enjoyed the Beatles too, but always preferred the Stones style and their "bluesy influence." Ugotthesilver liked "Shattered" best of the Stones songs he first heard on his own radio, becoming a fan ever since. After "The Last Time" blared out of his little transistor radio, a fan said "he never went back to the bubblegum AM-radio "normal" music ever again.

"I heard my first song in the womb," said a fan, when her mother pressed her headphones to her growing stomach. She couldn't answer which song was her favorite in the beginning and can't answer now because she "has too many favorites." In contrast, one guy heard "Wild Horses" coming home from a swimming meet in high school, finding it on the album *Stripped* in the library two years later. IRLTS heard "Shattered" in college, and immediately started doing "an impression of Mick" singing the song. Was he any good? IRLTS answers with a song lyric from "Streets of Love": "I must admit, the awful truth, I was awful bad."

These stories represent the range from youngest to oldest audience members among the online fans, relishing their memories whether from the distant past or not very long ago. My own nearly life-long love of the Stones is very much like their passion for the band, struck hard with the first songs I heard.

"Satisfaction" won out of 81 fan-generated choices when people at Shidoobee answered my online question about the first Stones song they really liked. Some mentioned more than one song but only the first was counted in the tally. The vote was varied, though. In the top ten, after "Satisfaction" and "It's All Over Now" at number two, a few songs tied for third most popular, including "Time Is On My Side," and "Let's Spend the Night Together," both songs performed live on the Ed Sullivan shows in the States, and "Shattered." "Shattered" is the song in which the name of the Shidoobee fan club appears, in the lyric in the last stanza: "huh Shadoobie, my brain's been battered," or "huh Shidoobee," in another written rendering of the sounds. Two fourth-ranked tunes, with four votes apiece included "Gimme Shelter," noted as an all-time favorite of some fans, even if they liked it later on making it ineligible for their first remembered, first preferred song. Also fourth was the tune that had such an impact on me when I got pushed out of the parental nest, "Get Off of My Cloud."

If they were too young to buy their own vinyl, tapes, or CDs, the fans depended upon their parents or often, their older siblings for continual access to the Stones. With recorded music, fans could indulge their taste by listening to a whole album or just one song as many times as they liked. With older relatives and then friends, fans had company agreeable to singing the songs and dancing to the music, and audiences for both. My nephew Max was only ten when I bought him the Stones song lyrics book. Because he knew much of the music from his dad's collection, he set into singing loudly, almost shouting: "Some girls give me chil'ren, I never asked for!" I heard his mother call upstairs, "Ma—a-ax! Stop!" Wincing and chuckling at the same time, I hadn't considered carefully which lyrics might be unsuitable for children. His mom took him to a live Stones show not too long after that.

Taking advantage of their older sisters' and brothers' collections, some fans put off buying their own copies for quite a while. A few raided their parents' recordings, usually their dad's stash. One fan told of his father naming him after Keith, a testament to the parent's devotion to the guitarist and the band. Others found their interest surging after listening to the Stones at home, prompting them to purchase their own singles or albums.

Because of the ages of the fans and the specific time period of exposure, from under ten years old to pre-teen to early or late teenager, the actual recordings bought first varied quite a lot. Fans here heard or bought albums from 1964's *12 x 5,* 1965's *December's Children, High Tide and Green Grass,* and then *Got It Live if You Want it,* from concert recordings, released in 1966. The late sixties and early seventies brought *Let It Bleed, and Sticky Fingers,* with the much-loved live albums of that time period, *Hot Rocks and Ya Ya's.* Fans bought another compilation from their shows, *Love You Live,* and the studio recordings of *Some Girls* and *Tattoo You* into the late seventies and early 80's. The same fan named after a Rolling Stone bought his first recording as a present for his father in 1994, *Voodoo Lounge.* Many started with singles, both for their lesser cost, one recalling, "I was a poor broke student!" and the popularity of 45s back then. These included "Get Off Of My Cloud," "Jumping Jack Flash" and "Honky Tonk Women" of the 1960s. A male fan explained his reasoning on first going for the singles before he finally plunked down the money for a whole album:

I pretty much just bought the "45s" when I was really young, without a lot of money, and thinking that the only decent songs a band produced were released on "45s" and played on Top-40, AM radio. The first album I ever bought was Beggar's Banquet in 1968 when I was 16 and starting to discover FM radio. I was totally blown away by Sympathy for the Devil -- staying up for hours just to hear it one more time on the radio. After a few nights of that, I plunged for the album.

He thought back on that period of his life, marveling at his own daring to invest in "a bunch of other songs on the LP that I had never heard before." He bought them because the single song, "Sympathy for the Devil" had affected him so much. He tuned in to two radio stations at once so he could hear broadcasts of baseball games "while spinning the dials of another trying to find a rock station that would be playing "Sympathy."

Andrea Baker

Introducing the Online Fan Groups, their Leaders and Members

The internet allows fans from all over the globe to commune online in their passion for the Stones. Even so, each group has a geographical base at least somewhat related to the leader who started it. While there is overlapping membership, with some fans belonging to two or three groups, most have a home group, a community that claims their strongest allegiance. "It's Only Rock 'n Roll" or "IORR" has the largest number of members and readers, outside of rollingstones.com, which dropped its sign-ups and discussion board a few years back. IORR is one of the longest running of the main Stones sites, following the hard copy magazine of the same name that the leader Bjornulf Vik (bv) of Norway has published since 1980, also called The Rolling Stones Fan Club of Europe. In its online form, IORR.org began in 1996, with news of albums and tours, although it didn't include the discussion forum "Tell Me" until 2000, shortly before StonesDoug started Shidoobee. IORR posts links to the other three major Stones groups covered in this book, as well as to other fan sites in Europe. The website contains concert reviews of each show on a tour, and has special forums for the selling and trading of tickets and "imports" or recordings of live shows and merchandise.

While the largest percentage of members are Americans, IORR has a high concentration of fans outside of the U.S. and Canada, mainly from Europe, and also including Australia, New Zealand, and Central and South America. I had the the chance to interact with Bjornulf offline a bit during the *50 and Counting* tour, and I bought an IORR t- shirt, a limited edition garment designed by a member of the IORR group, sent to people directly from Bjornulf's residence. He goes to almost all of the European shows on each tour, as well as many of the shows in the U.S. and elsewhere. When I went to London in August 2007 for the closing of *A Bigger Bang,* I flew from the States to attend two of three shows at the O2, meeting up with people from several different countries and fan groups. Many of the fans I encountered were from

22

IORR, showing up at largely spontaneous pre-concert gatherings at bars close to the venue and to the main fan hotel, or in the bar inside it.

Stonesdoug (Doug Potash) started Shiboobee in 2001, when discussion became contentious in an AOL group formed to discuss the Stones. His site is the locus of the beginning of this fan project, and contains many of the fans that talked to me in-depth, about two-thirds (66%) of the total participating in complete interviews. Shidoobee is the first online community for Stones fans that caught my attention. I began posting on it almost immediately after joining and read it frequently. It is more informal than IORR is in some respects, with more personal back-and-forth joking, possibly because more fans have met each other face-to-face while going to concerts and pre-parties. The main moderator, Stonesdoug, sometimes helped by oldkr, (Keith Walmsley), a man in his twenties originally from the UK, shows a higher degree of tolerance for patron kidding and insults than Bjornulf, who has more detailed rules about acceptable kinds of posts. At Shidoobee, off-topic discussions on matters other than the Stones can spring up anywhere, some eventually closed or redirected by a moderator or another fan. There is a separate forum called "Non-Stones News and Info" for information on other bands and events. With only one main discussion forum, Bjornulf insists that all non-Stones threads have the name "O/T" in their titles. At Shidoobee, there are whole sub-forums for non-Stones-related material, such as "Fans of the Rolling Stones-non-Stones articles". Also Shidoobee has more personal forums such as one for celebrating people's birthdays, and it provides other separate forums for people who need emotional support or other kinds of help, and for gatherings of Stones fans outside of regular scheduled shows of the band.

Now in Annapolis, Maryland, Doug has lived on the East Coast since he started his online fan group, and has arranged and attended get-togethers regularly with fans before Stones concerts and for bands that cover the Stones. He is a singularly personable man, an extravert who, offline, greets anyone new to Shidoobee with a bear hug and welcoming words.

The phrase I've heard most often about Stonesdoug from people who've met him is "He's great!!" My research focused on Shidoobee, with the early questionnaire, the most intensive observation, and, as noted, the largest number of interviews. In this chapter and beyond, any further comparisons between sites occur mainly between Shidoobee and IORR, with some among all the groups, including the next two.

Started in1998 by people from Northern Ireland (Gazza/Gary Galbraith), Mexico (Voodoochile/Gerardo Liedo) and Denver, Colorado (Jaxx), Rocks Off (RO) is the smallest of the three discussion boards, with over 800 members registered. RO seems to have proportionately more guests than the other groups, people who don't post but just read. The irreverent tone of RO comes from its membership, supported by the leadership. There is even more joshing, jesting and personal slamming, pseudo or real, here than at the other two places, giving the feel of an in-group. A small band of posters, about twenty or so interacts during an average week, and many have met in person at Stones shows. Using a list of dates like Shidooobee, RO routinely celebrates birthdays of members, whereas IORR brings up someone's special day only when a member starts a topic to observe the particular occasion. RO has a link to the "news" section of IORR and Gazza and Stonesdoug cooperate to post the set lists from each show in Europe and the US during the tours. Of the three founders of RO, I've met Gazza, a warm and accommodating person, and spoken to Voodoo Chile by phone, who like Gazza, is very friendly and supportive of this fan project. Aside from his own board, Gazza posts quite a lot on IORR, where he relinquishes his host role to that of knowledgeable fan.

Stonesdoug applies a looser hand in moderating his site than Bjornulf, as noted, and Gazza and his cohorts employ perhaps the least control on the three public sites. The website guidelines for Shidoobee and IORR both prohibit discussion of religion and politics, and Shidoobee discourages lengthy debates of the merits of the Beatles and the Stones, and comparison of former guitarist Mick Taylor and Ronnie Wood.

Stonesdoug suggests that anyone who finds "insulting or derogatory" posts write to him. Similarly, Bjornulf says he will not tolerate "offending or personal" posts and requires "respect" by members on his board. He forbids "derogatory" writing, with Stonesdoug, and also "offensive and unacceptable" language. He adds further written direction to people who find their posts deleted or their access denied: write to him showing you understand why and he will reinstate you. If not, he won't do it. Stonesdoug has banned people too, usually letting them back in after a time, and after some communication by private messaging or email.

Most fans who contributed to the interviews in this project not found in the groups above belong to Undercover (UC), a private email list. With permission from the leader, I have conducted interviews with some members, and occasionally describe the general features of the list, but don't quote from members there without a person's individual consent. This group started early on, in 1992, becoming the first Stones group online among the four. After an opportunity to work in Silicon Valley, and happening upon a book on the Stones recording sessions, Steve Portigal asked his IT department back at the University of Guelph to set up a mailing list for fans. UC fans lean toward the "tweediest," including Martin Elliott, the author of a string of volumes that have compiled and annotated the Stones known recordings throughout the years. Elliott's first book in his ongoing series, *The Rolling Stones: Complete Recording Sessions 1963-1989* (1990) prompted Steve to begin thinking of how to locate others with similar interests and how to communicate with knowledgeable fans. Some members of this group get together in person, perhaps as much as those from Shidoobee, most often meeting in Northern California, the current home of the founder. They've had gatherings near Clarksdale, Mississippi, in honor of the blues history of the U.S., and in 2010, I was able to participate in that. In common with the other fan groups, the bulk of posters are North Americans, while some of their membership lives in Europe and elsewhere outside of the States, in places such as Central and South

America. They call themselves "the Glimmers", after the Glimmer Twins, a label for Mick and Keith. Steve says his group is really more about "the people" on the list than the tracking of information per se.

Other fan boards mentioned by people interviewed are the Stones Vikings of Sweden, with its president MickieJaggeroo (Vilhelm Ortendahl), the Forty Licks Fan Club from the Netherlands, and the now defunct Belgian Rolling Stones Fan Club, founded by Chris (coowouters), a member of Shidoobee, and others. Representing a fraction of all of the clubs throughout the world, these clubs have websites, but primarily function to hold social events for their members, sometimes with cover bands. Until 2010, there was also the international newsletter *Stones Planet* of The Rolling Stones Fan Club Office of Scandinavia and the UK, first begun back in 1964 before becoming international in 1999 with its accompanying website. The RSFCO disbanded in late 2009, halting its paper publication along with the website. There are also fan-run sites centered on the admiration of individual band members, public and private, such as The Keith Shrine, "a page dedicated to the human riff and his followers" run by Blue Lena since 1996, and a private chat place for Keith fans called Voodoolounge.

Blue Lena (Tamara Guo) has The Keith Shrine, a website and now a Facebook page too. She edited and wrote for *Stones Planet* in its years of operation until 2009, and her shrine is still connected to Stones Planet Brazil and Stones Planet Belgium. She regularly attends events for fans, and is respected and liked by many. In the last several years, people have joined groups on social networking sites such as Facebook and MySpace to announce their fandom of The Rolling Stones and individual members and their back-up singers and musicians, along with ties to cover bands. On Facebook, people post pictures with band members, and keep in contact with other fans about their non-Stones interests as well as engaging in Stones-related banter with fans in their personal friendship networks. Shidoobee and some of the other online clubs have added Facebook pages for communication with fans who like social media.

Most of the fans who completed full interviews are from Shidoobee, 66%, and 34% are from other fan sites, a little more than half of those from IORR, with the rest split between RO, UC, and European fan boards. Some fans read and post at more than one group, but usually claim a stronger affinity for one over the other. A couple of fans go on Gasland, pointing to it as a supreme source of Stones lyrics. Represented in all the age groups, the largest proportion of fans, 82%, are in their forties and fifties, with 14% under 40 and 4% over sixty years old. Levels of education vary from high school to Ph.D. The dominance of men in this study may partly reflect who was willing to give me, the female author, an hour or so of time to talk. More objectively, viewing fans in these groups on the internet shows that this gender representation is quite close to the sex of active online fans, although the proportions of audience members who show up at concerts may skew more toward an equal balance.

The leaders of the four major fan groups with people I spoke with, following the majority of fans interviewed, are all in their forties or older, except one, with long histories of fandom in their listening habits and concert attendance. I have interviewed both leaders of Shidoobee, Stonesdoug and oldkr, the two active leaders from RO, Gazza and Voodoochile, and the sole head of UC, Steve Portigal. Others interviewed include Blue Lena, MickieJaggeroo, and two leaders of Dutch and Belgian fan groups. Although I did not have the opportunity to interview Bjornulf for the project, I have read his posts at IORR and observed that discussion board since 2005. Two of the current leaders and founders of the four groups are from Europe, one from Mexico, and three, including the newer, younger leader, oldkr, are from the States, although four of the five have gone to concerts in continents outside their home areas. What I found in England at two of the three final concerts of *A Bigger Bang* tour (2005-2007) was that people from all the fan communities came together, much more than at the U.S. shows, including most of the leaders. People from all the online communities comingled in the bar at the main hotel, the St. Giles in London, and at two other bars, the Jack Horner close to the hotel, and The Pilot Inn near the O2, frequented before the shows. Aside from the noteworthy occasion of the end of the tour, knowing that three of the four Rolling Stones still make their homes in Great Britain and began their performing career in the London area helps make sense of the concentration of varied fans at the London shows.

These planned and spontaneous Stones concert pre-and post-parties in London, fan events in Las Vegas, New York, New Jersey, Berkeley, California, and Clarksdale, Mississippi, and yearly Shidoobee shindigs in places in the eastern U.S, most often in Wildwood, New Jersey have let me meet many of the fans I first encountered in the online communities. Adding the fans I first interacted with at the Clapton's Crossroads Guitar Festival in Chicago and at a Belgian Stones fan club day, both in 2007, I have met in person nearly two-thirds (62%) of the 103 fans fully interviewed for the project. Meeting some before interviewing them and some after, this percentage is doesn't count the fans who provided select information on the *50 and Counting Tour*.

CHAPTER TWO:

"2000 LIGHT YEARS FROM HOME: THE STONES AND OTHER BANDS FROM THE COUNTERCULTURE TO CYBERSPACE"

"I've always been childishly fond of the flower power years...1967...I really love *Satanic Majesties*." (Baboon Bro)

"Sex, drugs, and rock 'n roll!" No one seems to know who coined the phrase, although Ian Drury wrote a song with a similar title in 1977 that further popularized it. The saying originally applied to aspects of the "counterculture," a set of behaviors and attitudes among young people that emerged first in the 1960s in the U.S. and parts of Europe. The term counterculture encompasses a complex of lifestyles, attitudes and political stances that sprang up to oppose the mainstream, borrowed from the sociologist Milton Yinger who first applied it to urban gangs in the 20th century. Most of the fans quoted in this book were too young to hear the band live in the heart of the counterculture era. Though exact dates differ, here the estimated pre-counterculture in England and the States is 1962-1964, the peak years of the counterculture with widespread awareness and practices involving new drugs, new forms of intimate relationships, and new political stances from 1965-1970, and the later counterculture 1971-1975 or so, coinciding roughly with the end of the Vietnam War. The overt anti-establishment influences trailed on through the seventies in Europe and the States, and over to other places such as the Eastern Bloc countries into the 90s, with vestiges continuing today in diverse locations.

The countercultural phenomenon included two major wings, the so-called "hippies" who initiated change in appearance and lifestyle and the "activists," the politicos who protested the Vietnam War and backed causes such as student rights. While some gravitated to one or the other pole of interest, there was much overlap in the groups. Both backed the notion of "peace" and often wore the symbol in their jewelry and on their clothing, with hippies adding "love and happiness" to peace, applied to personal relationships and their overall approach to life. Music, notably rock music, along with pop and folk, provided the backdrop for both groups. Rarely if ever, before or after, did the music and lyrics of a time period reflect so instantaneously the themes and the actual happenings of an era, most clearly within the works of singer/songwriters such as Phil Ochs, Bob Dylan, and Crosby Stills Nash and Young (CSNY), and also in the lyrics of the Beatles, the Dead and the Stones. Within their own everyday worlds, you'd hear people speaking later on about "the soundtrack of my life," marking important events with particular songs or albums.

Many have written extensively over the years on all aspects of the counterculture with a variety of perspectives and motives. For early examples, see Ken Keniston's analyses of disaffected youth, and the "young radicals" (1965, 1968), and, perhaps most famously, Theodore Roszak on the "making of a counterculture" from 1969. My intent is to place The Rolling Stones into context with other bands and their fans, from their beginnings at the pre- dawning of the counterculture and their part in it, to their place in the shift to the cyber-age. The Stones, along with the Beatles and the Dead manifested strands of countercultural hippie themes, of sex and drugs, and occasionally their lyrics showed political leanings. Years later, beginning with access to the web and personal computers, for the mutual benefit of bands and fans, social media could distribute information about musical groups among their acolytes, and let them exchange ideas and social support, faster, and to many more people than in pre-internet days.

You Get What You Need

Sex and Drugs in the Counterculture

The sexual revolution of the sixties applied mainly to the increased activity of women partnered with men, who were having much more premarital sex than before, without having to take on the label of slut or whore, as in the past. The widespread distribution of "the pill" in the years after its initial FDA approval in 1960 contributed to the sexual freedom of the times. Helping along the more open and frequent sexual relationships among young people was the practice of cohabitation. Without benefit of marriage, for the first time in the U.S., couples could move in together, setting up housekeeping. Friends, too, any number of them, could live in a common residences, unlike before, when only relatives, those with formal kinship ties, could typically share a home or apartment. Not only did cohabitation eventually become the norm for couples considering marriage, but also sexual activities that people formerly viewed as kinky or beyond the pale took their place in ordinary sexual repertoires. Oral sex for both men and women became almost mandatory activities. Illustrated by the lyrics of CSNY, some experimented with casual sex, "Love the one you're with," or multiple partners, "Why can't we go on as three?"

Masters and Johnson's clinical work and writing boosted the idea of women's inherent sexuality, moving the culture away from the popular stereotype of the frigid female. With their clinical research on sexual function and dysfunction in their St. Louis laboratory, they found that with proper and often extended stimulation, at least some women could easily have multiple orgasms per session. For many women, the "big O" often had proven elusive before this "discovery," years before writers described the G-spot. A decade or so after Masters and Johnson, in the early to mid seventies, Shere Hite talked to thousands of women, indicating that 70 per cent of them needed more than sexual intercourse to achieve orgasm, exploding the so-called myth of the vaginal orgasm. With manual and oral stimulation, particularly of the clitoris, added securely to the repertoire of foreplay, women's increasingly

31

acknowledged sexual desire could result in physical fulfillment and release. Masters and Johnson graphed this process of sexual stimulation and release they found in their St. Louis lab studies, showing a more gradual arousal and a much longer plateau before climax for females than males. With this knowledge, more women could add physical gratification to the emotional intimacy and cuddling traditionally valued and appreciated by females.

Women found themselves divided in the feminist movement over whether to emphasize their now explicitly recognized sexuality or to downplay this aspect in favor of critiquing the notion of woman as sexual object. Meanwhile heterosexual men who had learned about technique and results from the research liked that more women were engaging in sex with less guilt and more pleasure. People no longer assumed the commitment of marriage, while women joined men in valuing both sex and affection in their enduring relationships. Females even began to take the initiative in the process of pairing up, breaking away from old patterns of submission and passivity in courtship.

Gay liberation followed the contemporary feminist movement, after the Stonewall incident in 1969 when gay people protested the arrest of patrons at a bar in New York City who were corralled by police simply for their sexual preference. The practice of homosexuality did not become legal in most U.S. states until the early 1970s, after the American Medical Association reversed its diagnosis that homosexuality was a disease of arrested development.

Young people crossed sexual boundaries and indeed, had more "satisfaction" in their sexual activities, with less guilt, more information, and more partners in this pre-AIDS landscape. After the Stones hit song, a reporter asked Mick Jagger at a press conference captured by Albert and David Maysles in their 1970 film *Gimme Shelter*, "Are you any more satisfied now" than you were before? He replied with a question of his own before answering: "Do you mean, sexually or philosophically?"..."Both." ..."Sexually, satisfied, philosophically, trying."

Both the Beatles and the Stones were greeted by screaming fans when they first toured in England and the States. Indeed, films and live reports testify that the screams often overwhelmed the sounds of the musicians. Only Frank Sinatra had previously elicited similar teen reactions when appearing in public. Doing sets of very short duration by today's standards, the band members likely didn't see the point of playing longer shows. The female fans predominated in both the Beatles and Stones audiences at first, but the Stones soon attracted more males while holding the girls' attention. They band members on stage commented over the years that they felt a real surge of female sexual tension. Desire was coming to the fore, rather than merely the more innocent romantic crushes on male pop stars like Frankie Avalon and Fabian. The blues music that undergirded the whole British invasion of bands in the 60s, especially the Stones, grew from the earthy urges depicted by black American musicians of the Mississippi Delta. When talking with American journalists, Keith Richards has noted, ironically: we took your music and gave it back to you.

Song lyrics picked up where the blues and early rock 'n roll left off to reflect and affect the counterculture. From the innocent wish of the Beatles' "I Wanna Hold Your Hand" to the Stones' bold invitation of "Let's Spend the Night Together," sex and music blended more overtly than ever. Instead of a playing a backdrop of songs crooned by Sinatra and Tony Bennett, or caressed by Ella's silky sounds while dining by candlelight, people discussed the best sound tracks to play when having sex.

Mick Jagger possessed an openly sexual demeanor and sang seductively about black prostitutes ("Brown Sugar") and perhaps most famously, as mentioned earlier, about trying to achieve "Satisfaction." Not since black blues artists such as Muddy Waters' ode to his mojo and lyrics about jellyrolls had such explicitly sexual lyrics proliferated. The early rock hits "Shake, Rattle and Roll," "Great Balls of Fire" and even more, Little Richard's "Good Golly Miss Molly" had tantalizing phrases that came close. DJs at white American rock stations rarely played Little Richard, Chuck Berry or Bo Diddley, until the British rockers who became well known by good-sized audiences drew attention to their influence. Censorship of Stones lyrics penned by Jagger/Richards progressed from "Let's Spend the Night Together" on their 1967 Ed Sullivan appearance through recent years. Including "Satisfaction," their songs contain countless sexual references, such as in the lyrics to "Honkey Tonk Women," "Midnight Rambler," "Beast of Burden," and "Some Girls," with lyrics detailing what various ethnic and racial groups of women really want from their men, sexually and romantically. "Rough Justice" (2005) complains, "Now I'm just one of your cocks." For the 2006 Super Bowl half-time show and a concert in China the same year, officials identified songs with sexually provocative expressions, removing them from the set lists to preserve their notions of decency.

The androgyny of Mick Jagger and others during the seventies brought questions of bisexuality and gay identity to the rock performers. In most cases, any suspected experimentation with casual lovers soon resolved into stable relationships with female partners. Mick's ability to excite both men and women extended his appeal and broadened the popularity of the band, while adding to the Stones' controversial image.

Though the two bands were portrayed as rivals within the "British Invasion," John Lennon spent a lot of time with Mick and Brian Jones. The Stones' publicist Andrew Loog Oldham, who had worked for the Beatles first, punched up the media perception that the Stones embodied the rebellious "bad boys" of rock and roll, the counterpoint to the Beatles more mainstream "mop tops." Keith notes in his autobiography *Life* that the Beatles had the "white hats," so what was left? "The black hats." Whether the drugging and sexual behavior of the two supergroups was all that different is another question. Through information in journalistic accounts and self-reports, individual Stones were probably consistently more extreme, fitting the image of the rock and roller life style imitated by legitimate rockers and wannabes ever since.

A hallmark of the counterculture was the hallucinogenic drug, added to the cornucopia of American mind-altering substances of the 20th century, such as the cocktail and the tranquilizer, not to mention the ever-present cigarette and cup of coffee. The generations divided along pre-marijuana, LSD, and mescaline age groups versus post-psychedelic drug availability and ingestion. Amphetamines and depressants or "uppers" and "downers," previously prescribed mainly for dieting and sleeplessness also circulated casually among the youth of the counterculture. Cocaine and heroin came later to the middle classes, either too expensive or considered too dangerous for most outside of rock musician circles.

Tim Leary turned from Harvard professor into high priest of acid before and after his experimentation with LSD-taking by Cambridge residents led to his firing. He appeared on American television in white robes, chanting the famous words "Turn on, tune in, and drop out." Parents of young people did not relish the prospect of their progeny doing any of those things. They weren't sure what tuning in or turning on meant. The thought that their children would drop out of their college experiences, often financed by the parents, worried them greatly. I remember watching Leary with my own parents in the one-TV household common for the times, and they seemed shocked, in contrast to my own fascination.

Returning to the music, the Grateful Dead began as the Warlocks, playing their first show of blues and Stones covers in May 1965 in San Francisco. They soon changed their name, reflecting a popular book of the counterculture, *The Tibetan Book of the Dead.* The Dead became the favorite of "heads" and represented, through the leader Jerry Garcia, not only the hedonistic leanings, but perhaps more importantly, the spiritual aspects of the counterculture, including communalism through strong group bonding and pacifism. Care of the earth and respect for its resources grew out of this ideology, culminating in Earth Day and continued in the conservationist practices of the annual Burning Man Festival. Better living through chemistry was co-opted from Dow Chemical to indicate the pleasure of the highs that triggered the feelings of universal brotherhood and sisterhood, reflected back into the everyday lifestyles. Fans of the Grateful Dead formed caravans to follow the band's tour from city to city, and would sell, trade and give away paraphernalia related to the band and the counterculture. Audience members were usually tripping on LSD at their concerts and passing joints around, behaviors shared with most of the band members.

As young people scrutinized song lyrics printed inside albums of the time, drugs became a well-known theme. Noteworthy is that bands including the Beatles and others have nonetheless denied drug-oriented interpretations of their lyrics. In any case, "Girl we couldn't get much higher" stands as a crucial line of the band that named itself after Aldous Huxley's experiences with hallucinogens in *The Doors of Perception.* The Doors combined the imagery of both drugs and sex in their popular tune "Light My Fire." As well as the drug-based lyrics, in this period, drug use among the listeners and often the creators accompanied the music. People selected music to play that best matched the type of drug ingested. Jimi Hendrix went with acid very well, as did the Doors. Much of Jefferson Airplane mixed well with psychedelic and other drugs, most obviously demonstrated by their classic *Alice in Wonderland*-based "White Rabbit": "one pill makes you larger, and one pill makes you small..." Young people started to talk about what they were listening to when certain events in their lives took place, associating particular songs with special times, going well beyond couples' traditional marking of a favorite ballad for "our song." Because "album-oriented" rock began to replace very short tunes, "hits" heard in isolation, people valued whole albums produced by their preferred groups as well as individual songs. They habitually shared them with their friends and new acquaintances by playing them on their turntables, and lending or trading their vinyl records.

The Grateful Dead's mantra in "Truckin," "What a long strange trip it's been," describes drugs and life on the road, and the railroad engineer "Casey Jones" who's "driving that train, high on cocaine" are obvious references to mind-altering substances. The dealer's rant in "Candyman" details the lure of drugs, although older blues songs highlighted the title character's sexual attributes and appeal to women. A large part of listening to the Dead's songs in concert celebrated the ubiquitous effects of acid that often flowed freely among the band members and the audience. The followers of the Dead traveled around the U.S. and elsewhere to see their band in concert. Their gatherings many hours before the show, campers in circles of tents around the outdoor venues became legendary, a part of the show itself, an essential experience.

The Beatles' experimentation with LSD and other hallucinogens affected their lyrics and music. Lennon and McCartney have claimed that the letters in "Lucy in the Sky with Diamonds" were a coincidence, although they inserted much psychedelic imagery in the lyrics. John clipped the title from a drawing of his son's classmate called Lucy O'Donnell, and Paul agrees that they didn't notice the letters in the title until fans later pointed them out. "Day Tripper" combines the title allusion to LSD with the sexual activity of a female "teaser" who "took" the songwriter "half the way there" and only did "one night stands." In "Happiness is a Warm Gun," heroin use is implied by "I need a fix" because I'm crashing, and "bang, bang, shoot, shoot" with sex mixed into lyrics such as when I put "my finger on your trigger." Clearly psychedelic are the closing bars of "A Day in the Life" with the London Symphony Orchestra's chords crescendoing to the conclusion. The whole *Sgt. Pepper* album signaled the start of the Beatles' psychedelic period, continuing through The White Album. Their contact with the Maharishi, Eastern philosophy and music had the most lasting impact on George Harrison, exemplified by his song "Within You and Without You."

Acid-soaked and pop art imagery filled the musical cartoon film *The Yellow Submarine*, the soundtrack following the Beatles quest to defeat "the blue meanies" who had drained Pepperland of its color. One version of the yellow submarine on a button showed the sub on a black background with flowers growing from the raised part or "sail" on top with a peace sign right below the stems. When the film came out, legions of fans, including me, immediately recognized the whimsical humor of the Fab Four in the script and the mod haircuts and clothes of their cartoon incarnations. We had that feeling not uncommon during the sixties and seventies, that our fantasies had come to life, that the music and art on posters and album covers and in film embodied our dreams of merging media, of the synchronicity of realms of reality and imaginings.

Within the Stones catalogue, "Sister Morphine" most obviously points to familiarity with drugs, while other song lyrics contain references to drugs such as barbiturates in "Mother's Little Helper" and tripping to faraway lands in "2000 Light Years From Home." Busted for drug use more than once, Keith was an admitted heroin addict for ten years, Charlie had a cocaine problem, and Mick dabbled in various substances. Ronnie went to rehab centers to quit alcohol eight times, coming out of the last one with one of his longest sober periods thus far. He has said how nice it is to wake up focused instead of fuzzy, that he was hungover all the time when drinking. The Stones may have run the gamut of the range of drug users, from recreational experimenter to full-blown addict, and yet most of their lyrics are empty of obvious drug references. They are far better known for the sexually explicit phrases and themes in their lyrics and song titles, and in the sexual force in the music and performances.

From the start of white rock and roll, a hybrid of country music and the blues from the black community, it has exemplified rebellion. Even today, as rock is increasingly commodified for example, providing a band's music free with purchased objects that represent it, rock music still channels youthful energy of each generation. Many parents stick with the music they heard when they were young, and the boomers were fortunate to grow up with quality music that has lasted, including songs that mirrored the events of the times.

Politics in the Counterculture

Embodying the popular idea that music is "the universal language," artists of the counterculture like CSNY combined the hippie and political branches of the counterculture with the line "We can change the world." In their song, "Chicago," they asked if we believed in peace and justice after the beatings of the demonstrators against the Vietnam War in that city's 1968 Democratic convention.

"Woodstock Nation" of August 1969, epitomized the spirit of drugs, sex, rock and roll, and the cooperative vibes of the hippie counterculture. Four hundred thousand people gathered at Max Yazgur's six hundred acre dairy farm in the town of Bethel, overlooking the Hudson Valley in New York for a three-day weekend to celebrate the music. Joni Mitchell wrote her song "Woodstock" invoking the Garden of Eden after watching news reports and hearing boyfriend Graham Nash talk about the festival. Unfortunately, four months after the summer festival, fans attended the free concert at the Altamont speedway outside of San Francisco. Headlined by the Stones with Hells' Angels on security duties, for many, Altamont signaled the decline of the peace, love, and happiness era, with bad drugs and violence ending in the death of one person in the audience. On the political side, just a month before, in November 1969, those in "the Movement" drew more than half a million people to an anti-war demonstration in Washington D. C.

Clearly the times were "a-changing" a la Dylan and "there's something happening here," Mr. Jones, according to the Buffalo Springfield.

Shortly after seeing the photos in *Life* magazine, Neil Young of CSNY famously sat down to write the song "Ohio," released less than three weeks after the state's National Guard shot and killed four students and wounded nine others on the Kent State campus during an anti-war protest on May 4,1970. The recording's B-side was "Find the Cost of Freedom" by another band member, Stephen Stills. If Woodstock demonstrated the robustness of the positive vibes generated by the young people of the counterculture, the hippies, the Stones Altamont concert seemed to mark the beginning of the end of all that. Less than a half a year later, the Kent State anti-war protests and the four killings by the Ohio National Guard highlighted real danger for members of the political wing of the counterculture.

The Stones' most overtly political lyrics to date popped up in *A Bigger Bang's* "Sweet Neo Con," a 2005 critique of political leadership in the U.S., never performed in concert. Before that, and much better known are the words to the 1968 song "Street Fighting Man" which describes marches in the street and even a revolution, only to ask what can a boy really do, other than play rock and roll? Protest is ultimately futile. Keith and Mick have said over the years that they were musicians rather than change agents per se, despite the effects of their music, personas, and life styles on the youth of the times. John Lennon's 1968 lyrics for "Revolution" painted a negative picture of protest, calling it "destruction," counting himself "out" and later "out, in". However, after he met Yoko, the two staged their own "Bed-In" for peace in 1969 in Manhattan, writing "Give Peace a Chance" to explain what they were doing. His subsequent critiques of the Vietnam War after moving to New York City in 1971 made him Nixon's target for deportation, cementing his place in the anti-war movement. His song "Imagine" (1971) envisioned a utopian world without hunger or war.

You Get What You Need

Personal Reflections on the Counterculture

Older fans of the Baby Boomer cohort had personal experience with the counterculture in that they lived through the times, remembering when the Stones toured Britain, American and Europe in the 1960s. A fan in her sixties, not only did diane d of San Francisco attend Altamont, it was her second show, after a concert three months earlier in Oakland in 1969. She loved her first show, remarking that after a three-year absence from the States, the audience for the band was different, without "those screaming girls and boys."

> *I mean, I was in college when the stones first came on the scene and wasn't too interested in going to a show with a bunch of screaming teeny-boppers even if I liked the Stones' music...*

She was looking forward to her second concert, but Altamont was different. "It was a nightmare," says diane, born in the San Francisco Bay Area where she still lives.

Part of the backstage crew at Altamont, a fan now in her sixties, diane describes the Hell's Angels' behavior:

> *The Hells Angels were running amok--they were kicking people... My boyfriend found me and said "Lets get out of here". I said "Okay". We somehow got out of there. It was really a nightmare.*

Along with the Angels, the famously bad acid and rotgut red wine distributed widely at Altamont were blamed for some of the bad vibes, along with the very low height of the stage, allowing people easy access to jump up onto it with the band. More about diane's experience and review of the Stones performance, which she greatly enjoyed in spite of the circumstances, is in a later chapter on going to shows.

Fans around at the time refer to hippies and the cultural scene when they first heard the Stones. After the Democratic Convention of '68 where

41

police attacked youthful protestors with tear gas and clubs, 3DTeafoe from near Chicago pointed to the "huge generation gap." A year later, at fourteen, he was "hooked" when saw his first two concerts: "My mind was blown away by everything...my childhood was gone." 3DT became aware of the Stones' music early on seeing the band on Ed Sullivan. His older sister went to the shows in '65 and '66, bringing back the programs. She let her younger siblings into her room with "her idols plastered all over the walls...She had all the albums." Baboon Bro of Sweden describes his "childish" fondness for "flower power" and noticed a blossoming of the Stones creativity around 1967.

As far as values from the 60s, PartyDollMeg notes her "hippie years' but much like me, she was going to school, getting married and developing a career and so didn't attend a concert until the 90s. In contrast, Arthur, a fan now in his 50's began going to shows in the late 70s, toward the end of the counterculture era. Known offline as Michael Harrington, Arthur describes an episode at a concert where Mick and Keith spied him passing a joint in the stands at a show and Mick commented on it into the mic. Arthur observes that smoking marijuana isn't as common anymore since the audience has become more of a family-type gathering.

My own involvement was intense, yet at the fringes of the scene, never a full-blown hippie. Graduating from high school in 1964 I was at the oldest edge of the Boomer cohort. Turned out the Stones played Milwaukee that year, but I didn't pay much attention. My struggle for independence competed with my fear of finally growing up after an innocent childhood and early adolescence spent reading and studying. I listened to the opera and pop music of my parents, aside from what I heard on TV, from the shows we watched on our one TV like Ed Sullivan and for me, American Bandstand. There were those exceptional circumstances such as in junior high when I danced to teen music from a record player in someone's garage, and heard Chubby Checker and Bill Bailey a few times at high school dances. Only later did I hear Chuck Berry and Little Richard and their forerunners, the blues players. I do remember when Dylan's "Like a Rolling Stone" came blaring out of the portable radio I had in my room after I started college: talking to a female, he said she was on her own, unknown to anyone.

I lost my virginity at nineteen in that period when I lived away from home for the first time. I was exposed to the drug culture of the era, mainly with marijuana in joints rolled in cigarette papers or made from actual cigarettes, since most of us smoked nicotine prior to becoming marijuana users. Someone had a huge bong, with several tentacles for breathing in the "grass." Music accompanied all activities, that is, anything outside of work or school. Surrounding us in sound were Jimi Hendrix, the Beatles, the Jefferson Airplane, the Grateful Dead, the Doors, the Seeds, and the Stones, and at the end of the 60s, the softer sounds of CSNY and Joni Mitchell. The youth culture and counterculture flourished during a time of relative economic prosperity.

Because I didn't go away to college, I hung out in bars of my hometown, Milwaukee, Wisconsin, where head tripping and psychedelic music was coming in strong in the form of bands such as the Shaggs. They were playing at O'Brad's, the basement club on Locust, on the other side of the river from where I lived for a while. My neighborhood on the East Side, past the university near Brady Street became a major magnet for hippies later on. Young people were shacking up, some living together and even more spending good parts of the week sleeping over with another person, either a friend or often a sexual partner. Lines blurred between friendship and sex, as people explored a new freedom in forming relationships after leaving the parental nest. Most of my new friends were not in college, not residents of the dorm rooms, where some of my high school classmates lived. These dormitories were mainly out of town, many over at the main state campus, UW in Madison, and were gradually changing from one-sex residencies to coed during the 60s and 70s.

43

Men in my apartment building tried to figure out ways to get out of the draft. If their lottery numbers were low the danger of going to Vietnam was imminent. One person was arrested for selling marijuana and disappeared. I was dumbfounded—to me, she was just an ordinary part of our group, if a bit more flush with cash. I watched someone cover his apartment walls with black point, just because, literally enacting the song title "Paint It, Black." Shortly after moving back home, I found a steady boyfriend and we got married, after living together, "cohabitating" briefly. Our parents didn't know.

Until my divorce, during my grad school years, I had not tried acid. A fellow student decided to be my "guide" for my first magic carpet ride, not taking any LSD himself, selecting records for the duration. I remember the Doors, and Hendrix on "Purple Haze" and "Are You Experienced?" I wasn't. A few trips in the 70s and one or two follow-ups in the 80s constituted my career with acid.

Counterculture, Cyberculture and Rock n' Roll

Stewart Brand's *Whole Earth Catalogue* postulated the hippie creed of activity rather than passive spectatorship in its goal of "access to tools" so that people could shape their own environments and share what they discovered with other like-minded souls. Brand decided to bring a discussion format of his *Whole Earth Catalogue* of the late 60s and early 70s (and in other forms until 1988) into cyberspace online well before the World Wide Web or internet browsers. He started up a bulletin board called "The WELL," the letters standing for "Whole Earth 'Lectronic Link," still operating today. The initial culture of this online community grew out of three clusters within the San Francisco Bay Area: (1) the countercultural communalists, including tool builders and activists, (2) the programmers and early computer users, and (3) the Deadheads. Coining the term "virtual community," futurist Howard Rheingold has written extensively about the early years of The WELL (1993) since he joined in 1985.

From the start, The WELL had a whole conference on the Dead, with writers and techies contributing thoughts on the music and going to the concerts. The Dead epitomized the hippie side of the counterculture with its peace, love and happiness vibe. The band's ethos also idealized the communal, equalitarian values of youth of the period. Even today the Dead forum is advertised to potential subscribers of The WELL, along with other "hippie music" to draw people in. Their free version, "The Inkwell" allows nonmembers to read discussions with artists and authors, mainly featuring books about the counterculture or the digital realm.

As a member of the Boomer generation, I saw the *Whole Earth Catalogue* and its spin-off magazines, the *Co-evolution Quarterly* and *The Whole Earth Review.* I was studying the feminist movement in graduate school, choosing the topic of social movement organizations and ideology for my dissertation. I finally did buy the *Last Whole Earth Catalogue* when it came out in 1971 and there were several updates to that, ending in 1981. Because of a perceived deficiency in my technical skills and also a vision of the web as a free rather than a paid space, I never did register for The WELL. I sometimes regret not picking up on it after receiving the sign-up information and a thick booklet on how to get going with the membership. I knew some people began their online activities there, becoming charter members in the 1980s or joining a little later. They became well-respected "netizens," reporting about and analyzing online environments and interactions, developing full-time careers in such writing, inspiring me to pursue the research topics of internet relationships, identities and communities.

Online, bands found quick methods of advertising themselves freely, from webpages at first, announcing their scheduled gigs and new releases, and then through MySpace, the social networking mechanism that pre-dated Facebook. Solo performers and bands could collect friends or later fans on Facebook, with this built-in publicity among strangers, acquaintances and friends, who would share links to such pages with each other.

Even back before social media, through search engines such as yahoo.com, anyone could look up a band and find where people might write about it or talk about it. Print publishers began to establish online venues, such as when Keno and Bjornulf Vik started two of the first online spaces to celebrate and track The Rolling Stones. Like other online communities, people in these fan groups online began to meet to get to know each other, also bringing their offline friends and fellow fans online.

Unlike the Beatles or the Grateful Dead, The Rolling Stones are still performing as the original band with three of their founding members. The Stones took advantage of the internet, along with their fans. They had their site up for news and buying tickets, rollingstones.com, and their fans put up discussion groups starting in the late 1990s and early 2000s. During the *Voodoo Lounge* tour, Mick connected to the internet to broadcast the first songs that were seen and heard live online by a big-name band, welcoming fans listening online. Though not an actual webcast, the band employed the "Mbone," the streaming video technology of the times. Three years later, I heard "Start Me Up" live on my laptop at the beginning of the *Bridges to Babylon* tour, a thrill indeed. Each night, the Stones asked fans to pick a song to play live, to vote online for their favorite. Fans suspected a fast one when the some of the winners were announced, since they didn't believe those songs ranked with the most popular. However, this may have been the first tour anywhere that queried fans on their selections with the intent of importing them into the set lists on the day of the shows.

Long-time fans talk about how the ticket-buying process was completely different pre-internet. They phoned constantly to get past busy signals or cued up at ticket lines as early as allowed. Chapter Four tells how the internet has affected the whole experience of concert-going.

Giving the fans instant access to new and old music, to merchandise such as t shirts and mugs, and letting them buy tickets made online venues at first appealing and then almost a must for performers. The Stones' official site along with Clapton's and many others has sold fan club memberships, and distributed new music to them, as well as selling tickets before the general sales. In theory, the paid-up fans would then have better seats but this plan had not worked well more recently, said some fans. An online package called "Fan Asylum" provided benefits such as good seats to three shows, including a small club show, and transportation to the concert venues during the Stones *Licks* tour. Since then, the expense hasn't necessarily justified the rewards. I once sprung for a package and did sit on the floor about sixteen rows back but I had just as good a seat on the side buying through the Stones ticket site, though with a paid fan membership. Rollingstones.com finally abandoned its fan membership plans in favor of pre-sales of select seats for fans holding certain charge cards.

The Warner Brothers label Reprise decided their fourth album did not have enough commercial appeal, so rather than changing it, Wilco decided to release it on the internet in 2000. *Yankee Hotel Foxtrot* led to a sold-out thirty city tour, prompting Nonesuch records to buy back the rights from Wilco's leader Jeff Tweedy at three times what he paid Warner's. The internet made the band much more successful than it had been before. The net continued its role in the band's distribution when Wilco released *A Ghost is Born* three months before it came out offline. Rather than fighting file sharing, Wilco asked for donations from fans in return for downloading, raising money for charity.

Today it is almost more common than not for mainstream artists and alternative bands to release at least one track on the internet, often free to interested listeners. At the Rolling Stones site, the song "Rain Fall

Down" was available for download before the release of the 2005 CD *A Bigger Bang*, as were songs from the supplemented *Exile on Main Street*, re-released in 2010. With no announced release date, Beyonce dropped a whole album, brand-new on the internet, complete with videos for each of fourteen tunes in 2013.

Reviewing the trajectory of the many changes in the recording industry since online phenomena such as the downloading sites Napster and Limewire lies beyond the scope of this writing. Researchers at the Pew Internet and American Life Project tracked some of the changes in production and consumption within the music business, and, reactions of musicians and listeners. At one point (2009) they concluded that most musicians thought, on balance, that the internet had helped rather than hindered their careers. A Pew report assessing the scene looks at factors that may lead consumers to pay for music (2010) rather than to seek it out for free, in light of the major factors of cost, portability, mobility, choice of any song out there, and remixability.

CHAPTER THREE:

"HOPE YOU GET MY NAME: STONES FANS AND THEIR USER ID'S"

"I just went through a couple of Stones songs and decided that Honky Tonk Woman fit me. I just use it on Shidoobee." (HonkyTonkWom99)

Mickijaggeroo. HonkeyTonkWoman. Akissaway. CrossfireHurricane. Jason_the_Keithoholic. Rockman. LittleQueenie. RubyFriday. Promo. colditalianpizza, Stonesdoug. What's in a name?

Online, depending on the space, people can easily make up a name to describe their feelings, their personas, or their affiliations. With names that reflect their attachment to the band, many Stones fans online use IDs from particular songs or band members. Some just use the same online handles they've had in other contexts, or their real names, or a combination of a real name with a band-related name.

Our given names or first names can be changed if someone doesn't like the parental choice, often to a middle name or a nickname from childhood. Over the years, going by the name "Dick" has declined in favor of Rick, Rich, or the full name of Richard. Some go so far as to change their last name, if it happens to be a word that's fallen into derogative slang use, again, in the case of "Dick," or "Goober," just to name two examples. Fans of the Stones on the discussion boards can live out a fantasy by adopting the name of their favorite Rolling Stone, for example, usually with a twist to avoid duplication. Usually once a name is chosen, it is no longer available for someone else.

Names carry resonance through their sound and their meanings. Stones fans convert Stones lyrics and lore into their personal monikers. Once a fan becomes known for their name, others on the same fan board know not to take it for their own. If they do, even with a variation, they risk negative reaction and may have to replace it. Fans will come around to post that the name belongs to someone else, through tradition of its use. Choices of names vary by the customs of the fan community people initially join. These names are as colorful as the lyrics written by Jagger/Richards, or even more evocative with fans modifying the original band member names, song titles and words written for the music. Some names spring up through fans naming each other during interaction online or offline, while others just come into their heads when reviewing possibilities.

Unlike the tradition on Facebook for using real names, most Shidoobees have taken their cue from the founder, "Stonesdoug" (Doug Potash) and chose handles from the band name, song titles, or names of albums or band members. On the two other main public discussion boards, fans pick a greater variety of names, including their own nicknames from their everyday lives, again, following their leaders' preferences. One of the co-moderators at Rocks Off, "Voodoo Chile in Wonderland" takes his moniker from a Hendrix song. His partner at RO, "Gazza," has a variation of his real name that is commonly used as a nickname for "Gary" or any male name that starts with "Ga" in the UK. At IORR, the leader or "editor" signed up for a username of his first and last initials, "bv," and signs his posts with his given name, "Bjornulf" or his first and last names "Bjornulf Vik." At Undercover, many use their real names, including Steve Portigal, the UC founder.

Band-related Names, Band Member Names

A full head of streaked, straight hair that is light, turning to white, with his trademark forelock, his sparkling, wide-set blue eyes and a ready smile identify Doug Potash to the band and to many fans. Doug is known by his more familiar name of "Stonesdoug" as the head of a large, active, online fan group officially formed in 2000. This community holds pre-parties, post-parties and events outside of Stones' gigs for its members. His group's url is http://shidoobeewithstonesdoug. yuku.com, and his username illustrates his commitment to the band. His screen name is the model for others who combine a part of their real name with the band. The name was a gift from a friend who liked the music:

> *I was going to use a Stone's song as my moniker, but then remembered a girl I used to hang with in college named Julie. Whenever we were at a party, she would say "Stones, Doug, let's boogie" and we would get up and dance. So it seemed to fit and Stonesdoug was the first name I ever had on the internet.*

Before he recalled the phrase Julie had said to him, he had tried to think up some clever Stones name when he first signed up for AOL and formed a group there that was devoted to the band. Today people call him Stonesdoug, Doug, or sometimes "Shidoobee," for the online community he founded and named, after he and other fans split off from that early AOL group. Shidoobee comes from a lyric of the Stones song "Shattered," about life in New York City.

Everyone who meets him remembers Stonesdoug for his friendly inclusiveness, his robust greetings to all, to new Shidoobee members and old friends. In planning fan get-togethers throughout the years, Doug enjoys the "satisfaction I get out of it, of meeting people around the world who like the Stones as much as I do." He likes to mix fans that are already acquainted with "people they didn't know and make it comfortable for them." The band members and their back-up players have met Stonesdoug, a fan since the 1960s. He once sponsored Bobby Keys to headline a private concert for Shidoobees in Las Vegas during a Stones tour. Through Stonesdoug, a production coordinator on Martin Scorsese's film *Shine a Light* drew from Shidoobee fans to cast audience

51

members to attend rehearsals and sit close to the stage. In balance, filmmakers recruited fans from Bjornulf Vik's IORR to join celebrities in a fan film that opened shows on the *50 and Counting Tour.*

"Stoneszone9" came from Michaelene's screen name on AOL, before Shidoobee started. Eight others had taken the name before she arrived. She always used to hear a particular Philly radio announcer come on during a Stones tour saying, "We are in the Stones Zone, man." She often uses "being in the Stoneszone" when she needs an "excuse" for "not doing what she should" such as working, cooking or cleaning. A good-looking woman with long light hair and blue eyes, she notes that this excuse works better than just saying "I'm blond."

One set of popular names among fans includes band members' names or more likely, variations of them. Heading the Nordic Stones Vikings fan group, "Mickijaggeroo" (Vilhelm) is a large Swedish fellow with his trademark crop of brown hair, grown long, neck-length, often in bangs or parted over his forehead. He took his moniker from the 1987 movie, *Running Out of Luck*, a full-length eighty-eight minute film, or, as some see it, an extended music video for Mick's first solo album, *She's the Boss*. The film contains all the tracks on it, though in a different sequence, plus two Rolling Stones' tunes. The story begins with a fight between Mick and Jerry on their way to shoot a video in rural Brazil. The argument prompts Mick to take off on his own. He is kidnapped, turned over to the dominatrix owner of a banana plantation for her pleasure, and after he escapes, is robbed of his wallet while walking along a country road at night. The next part of the film was made into a stand-alone video in which Mick stops in at a local store to try to make a phone call for help. The small-town Latino shopkeepers have trouble recognizing the lead singer until he finds a Stones album in the store and puts it on their record player. Joined by a young boy, he dances to his own music, "Jumping Jack Flash." They chant, "Ah, Mickijaggeroo, Mickijaggeroo!" upon realizing who is in their store.

"JasontheKeithoholic" says he was always "the biggest Keith fan," prompting his old pal Jim "The Street Fighting Man" to bestow this nickname on him way back in 1981. Jason is on the younger side of fans, 37 at the time of the interview. He is grooming his two children, Caza and Jenson, to carry on the Stones tradition. They often sport t-shirts with band members on the front, and have accompanied Jason the K to yearly gatherings of Shidoobee fans and cover bands every Labor Day weekend. I met all three of them there, in Wildwood, New Jersey.

Jason, also known as "JJ" for Jason Joseph has an entity called "Keitholholic Records"; every hand-compiled release from his self-started company has "JJ" in the title. Keith was an object of adulation since the beginning of his Rolling Stones journey. He notes that since July 26, 1993, he has listened to at least one Rolling Stones song daily. Jason, a slender man with a lot of hair who can do a decent Mick Jagger imitation, is now his forties and married to his second wife. Of his two kids he says, "Jenson is a fan, but not like Caza and I. We did 'IORR.' It's on YouTube." Caza has been singing Stones songs with her dad for years, notably "Start Me Up" and "Honky Tonk Women," that they've performed in Wildwood on Sunday karaoke day. Caza is known at her school for her Stones apparel and accessories, including her Stones socks, her lunchbox, and the backpack decorated with a big Stones tongue.

Like Jason and Vilhelm, fans regularly choose names related to one of the band members, many times their favorite one, usually Mick or Keith, occasionally Charlie and perhaps Ronnie, although I've not seen his name as a user id. For example, Jaggrfn1 means just that, according to a woman who considers herself "Mr. Jagger's Number 1 Fan!" She had her favorite song "Ruby Tuesday," but later realized there was already a Ruby213 on the board, and she had no desire to "confuse people or copy someone's name," so she picked the new one.

Another female had a golden retriever/chow mix dog named Jagger she got from the SPCA in Annapolis, Maryland in 1996. The staff picked the name to match her love for Mick. She was on the Juno platform so wanted a name that fit with that. Her husband told her not to use her real name, and she came up with "jaggerlover." That way she decided whoever she is talking to could imagine "whether the Jagger is referring to my dog or Mick." She sometimes signs off on her comments with "Harriet, aka jaggerlover."

Virginia ended up changing her first username from SweetVirginia1, for the song title. She wants us to know, she's "not sure how sweet" she is, but I can say that to me and many others she is one of the sweetest fans around. She didn't want confusion with other women who had come up with variations on the name. Her new ID is "VirginiaJagger", but just for clarity, she was torn between that and "VirginiaRichards" before finally deciding on her first name with Mick's last name. According to Virginia, the riffmaster is equal to the front man, because, as she wrote in all caps, "YOU CAN LOVE 2 MEN EQUALLY."

Names from Stones' Songs and Slogans

On the distaff side, a slender, attractive female fan in her 40s, with a sculpted bone structure and shoulder-length thick hair varying in color at times from light brown with highlights to darker brunette, "Little Queenie" just "thought of something quickly." She and came up with a Chuck Berry song covered by the Stones in their early days, played at Madison Square Garden in 1969. She needed a name for IORR even though she never thought she'd be on it that much. For a while, during *A Bigger Bang* (ABB) tour, she found she "couldn't live without it," the IORR board. To explain her moniker, LQ notes, "i've always liked really old rolling stones and probably have a couple of bootlegs with little queenie on it." The song was recorded on the live album from 1971, *Get Yer Ya-Yas Out.*

After "trying a number of names and finding they were already taken," Annie wanted to "personalize" her choice somehow. She especially liked the *Some Girls* album, with a favorite track "Far Away Eyes," so she took off the plural of the title song, and then thought of adding her hometown in Canada to create the name of "SomeTorontoGirl." Toronto is often the home of rehearsals and opening gigs that kick off the band's North American tours. She can hardly believe she joined IORR over six years ago. Her tour activities have taken her to London at the O2 during ABB tour, and to NYC for Scorsese's premiere of *Shine a Light*. Both fans of the blues, we first met face-to-face at Eric Clapton's all-day Crossroads Guitar Festival in 2007 the first of two times he ran it outdoors at Toyota Park in Chicago. She is a witty writer on IORR, her posts in the mode of her creative name. I noticed STG when she joined a year or so after I did. For a long time she was one of the few females visible there, boldly bantering with the men, when I was still mainly lurking.

A generous fan who sends recordings of desired live shows to fans, Mr. Deeeee or "MRDEEEEE", all caps, has retired from the U.S space program in Florida. He originally had the more succinct handle with the one initial from the eponymous song title "Dancing with Mr. D" before a server change after a year or so at Shidoobee forced everyone to choose a new name. With the changed platform, someone else snagged his first choice "Mr.D." Since, friends were already calling him by the nickname online and offline, MRDEEEEE decided to add five "E's" so that people could tell the two Mister D's apart. Another fan likes to play with those "e's" often adding more of them to my name, appending them to the two I already have two, and then we both add them to his name. MRDEEEEE mentions how people offline often call him by his Stones name. Once he had put in a call to a co-worker of a friend who answered the phone asking, "Is this MRDEEEEE?"

From Chicago, "akissaway" drew her name from a famous line in the 1969 lyrics of "Gimme Shelter," asking for shelter from war that is "a shot away," and later switching to love that is "a kiss away." The lyrics address us listeners as "children," announcing the violence of war, rape, and murder back to war, and then in the last verse, turning finally to love again, only a kiss away." Rather than focusing on war "a shot away," the song ends on the soft, romantic note of a promised kiss, adding a bittersweet bite to the whole in its last lines. The juxtaposition of oppositional elements here recalls a slogan from the Vietnam era, "Make love, not war." This creative Midwestern fan found the words repeated in the final five phrases impressive enough to adopt it for her online identity, to label herself for other devotees. An avowed "Mick chick" or Mick Jagger aficionado, the statuesque akissaway has sleek brown hair with blunt cut bangs that show off her wide-set dark eyes. She designed her own version of Mick's face for her online personal avatar, a portrait in black and white.

One fan liking the song "Ruby Tuesday" goes by RubyFriday instead, to avoid duplications. RubyFriday is a man from Germany who laughs in agreement when asked if people often think he is a female. His case is similar to Edith Grove's in eliciting a high number of mistaken gender guesses. In the case of "RubyKel," a female combined a first name with the woman of the song. She has written that Ruby Tuesday is her dad's favorite Stones song. Some call her "Ruby" before they know her better, assuming it is her first name, but her own name is Kelly.

Taking his a cue from *The Saint* book series and later, the TV show of the same name starring Roger Moore, a future James Bond, "Saint of Me" was "looking for something cool," a name not taken by anyone else. He thought "Saint of Me," a relatively new song from the *Bridges to Babylon* CD, played live on the *No Security* tour would fit the bill. The user id "sounds risky daring and everything else that I'm not in my real life," he says, evoking the song's narrator who intersperses his story with martyred Biblical figures while refusing to be turned into a saint. His stick-figure avatar with a halo "makes me look thin," he jokes. Later we discussed how with one hand on his hip and the other jutted out, the avatar he found online looks something like Mick Jagger emoting onstage.

For a female handle, "Beast" or "The Beast" is quite a leap, to the point where people "tend to assume I'm a man, which is fine," says UK resident Sara, whose small stature is quite the opposite of her name. She does admire the song, "Beast of Burden." The word "beast" can apply to a woman as well as a man, if she is a particularly good competitor, as in "She's such a beast." For example, other players of Big Brother applied the term to the reality show contestant who excelled in physical and mental challenges, the glamorous Janelle Pierzina or "Jedi Jani." The Beast of IORR, Sara, sports a silver handcuff bracelet in honor of her favorite Rolling Stone Keith Richards.

Variations of a username are those that incorporate common sayings or slogans of band members or fans. These acronyms mean something to fans but not to outsiders. "IRLTS" is a name entirely made up by a guy whose initials stand for, "I really love the Stones." He explains, tongue in cheek, how he thought of the moniker:

> ...every name I tried to put in when I first joined was taken, and I was out of ideas - not unusual for me. That, combined with my total lack of creativity, led me to IRLTS, I really love the Stones. As East Coast Steve Holmes has pointed out to me, it also works for "I really love to ski," so it really encompasses the two loves of my life, the Stones and skiing...

A slender man employed in the medical field, IRLTS quickly adds his blonde wife Kate to the mix, his third love, and also a participant in Shidoobee online and his companion at offline gatherings.

"IGTBA" refers to Keith Richards' opening greetings during his solo set: "It's good to be anywhere," prompted by his life style earlier in his career, and the recurring predictions that he would die young. When interviewed about his notorious drug use of his past, Keith advises his audience: "Don't try this at home." IGTBA's nick took on an even greater resonance than usual after Keith Richards' fall in Fiji on a break during the ABB tour that resulted in serious head trauma requiring brain surgery. Keith repeats the phrase before his solo set, often with short add-ons to the theme of gratitude, such as "It really is."

IGTBA explains how he chose his moniker, observing that he really didn't intend to use it offline, didn't expect to meet anyone from the board, who would try to call him by his "unpronounceable screen name." He just wanted to "learn more about the ABB tour, so I picked a Keith acronym," one that would be "simple for me to remember." Now he meets a lot of Shidoobees at pre-parties and tells them who he is with his initials. When he was thinking of a name he recalled a friend who put a saying on his bike, and back then he thought he'd like to install Keith's pronouncement. When looking around at Shidoobee, he saw Keith-related names, so he said now is the time to use IGTBA.

A comment by Mick nicked from a live album leads to a nickname of a Shidoobee fan:

Arthur......got that one from the Stripped *album. Keith needs to start "Love In Vain" over, he says he hates it when he has to do that, and Mick kids him about "Arthur"..... maybe meaning arthritis.*

Only the hardcore fans familiar with *Stripped* or knowledgeable about intra-band banter can figure out how "Arthur" got his online name.

Stones' possessions and Stones' place names

A particularly evocative fan name is "Blue Lena." Fans of Keith Richards immediately recognize the name of a Bentley, a Touring Continental model he purchased in 1966 and then famously shared its backseat with Anita Pallenberg during the ride to Morocco the following year. He faced his first drug charge after police had raided his

You Get What You Need

Redlands estate in Sussex, accusing both Keith and Mick of possession of illegal substances. How did Keith come to name his car Blue Lena? Most obviously, the vehicle's deep blue paint struck him, probably echoing his favored musical form of "the blues" and he wanted to put that into the name. Added to that, the singer of jazzy torch songs who rose to fame in the U.S. in the 1940s, the beautiful Lena Horne sang such songs as "Stormy Weather," "Old Devil Moon," and "Love Me or Leave Me." She inspired The Rolling Stones guitarist and composer to grab her first name for his car. The two "l's" repeat in the two words, Blue Lena, in a mellifluous refrain.

The modern day Blue Lena is a special education teacher, and a writer who has co-edited the long-running, now defunct fanzine *Stones Planet*. A well-known fan of Mr. Richards, she has maintained her own website called "The Keith Shrine" since 1996, and a Facebook page called "The Keith Shrine by Blue Lena" with nearly 3,000 followers. While she doesn't favor blue clothing in particular, she does wear a lot of turquoise-blue jewelry. Fans who have seen her site recognize her offline by her shoulder-length, curly dark hair, occasionally worn straight these days, her wide, bright smile, and large aviator sunglasses. People call her "BL," or "Blue" or sometimes by her real name "Tamara," as well as "Blue Lena," In spite of rumor to the contrary, Keith says the car Blue Lena is still sitting in his garage.

A well-known now-retired gentleman from the west coast U.S., "Wembley21c" started out with Wembley99, named for the stadium in London, where he saw the Stones for the first time outside of his home country:

Sometime early in 1999, I felt I needed a new Stones-related screen name. About that time, the Stones announced they were rescheduling the previously cancelled British concerts from the year before (if you recall the fiasco regarding the British government trying to squeeze more taxes from their tour earnings). I had money saved and vacation time, and I got the brilliant idea of flying to London for a proper British style Stones concert, which, of course, was at Wembley Stadium. Such a trip was, for me at the time, a pretty big deal, so I got caught up in the moment and decided on Wembley99.

He wanted to update the moniker and he looked at other names, but he found that he and the Wembley name were so intertwined, he had to keep it, adding "21c" for the current century. Many people in the fan community call him that instead of John, his given name. Wembley muses that his screen name came to him in a sudden flash. "Looking back on it now, it strikes me that I did so a bit like Brian naming the group Rollin' Stones on the spur of the moment."

A notorious occasion with the bad vibes of a deadly knifing of an audience member, Altamont Speedway in the San Francisco area represents an important location of a Stones concert on December 6, 1969. The Maysles brothers immortalized the free rock festival on film in their documentary *Gimme Shelter.* One fan thought up that until that day, he "thought that the best things that had happened in music up to then were all the good times that went along with sex and drugs and rock & roll. His online name is "altamont 69" in memory of the "day in infamy in The Rolling Stones long history" of playing live music.

Other place names chosen by fans point to well-known meeting places or living spaces such as "Edith Grove," surprisingly a male fan's name. Like Beast, people often mistake him for the other gender. Edith Grove has a nice sound because of the two words corresponding to a first and last name of a person rather than, in reality, a street name in Chelsea where Mick, Keith, and Charlie shared a flat. One female fan has taken the online moniker of the neighborhood, "Chelsea," calling herself "Chelsea London". She says she chose the name because "Edith Grove (where it all began) is located in Chelsea, London. Plus, it sounds more feminine than 'Darford Kent!' :-)." Cheyne Walk and Nellcôte are among other residential landmarks in the Stones history, one a street in London where Mick bought a rowhouse, and the other the name of Keith's chateau in France where the band recorded the album *Exile on Main Street,* another place, a mythical location created for the recording. One fan at IORR has the name "Stargroves," the name of Mick's country estate on the southern coast of England during the 70s.

Blues and Rock Names

Living in Aspen, Colorado, the fan "BlindMellon" has a name related to his musical tastes and his own personal qualities. The popular Texas-born vocalist and blues guitarist Blind Lemon Jefferson in the 1920s included his disability into his nickname, along with the yellow fruit, his real given name, also listed in the census as "Lemmon." Lemon or Lemond is among names listed for common family names, in the historically Creole region extending into east Texas, as well as a slave name. Shidoobee member Marc Huley wanted BlindMellon because "it had the word blind in it," to describe his "partially sighted" vision. He sees shadows, making out shapes if not details.

He "remembered a skit by Cheech and Chong" called "Blind Melon Chitlin'" that was on their first album, 1971's *Cheech and Chong.* The comedy duo parodied a modern hippie on FM radio talking to very old blues artist, with Tommy (Thomas) Chong playing the bluesman. The bluesman Blind Melon falls asleep during the start of the interview, finally playing a bit of harmonica and singing a brief song that ends with scatological lyrics. BlindMellon thought it was "funnier than hell." Marc's nickname has no relation to the name of the U.S. '90s rock band Blind Melon, except for the common blues origin. He has heard of the band but never listened to their music. Marc's first choice was "Miss Amanda Jones," quickly discarded, to avoid the inevitable gender confusion, as a male participant. Having met BlindMellon and his wife Laura, a handsome couple, I find their humor and generosity gratifying, and his ability to get around with his cane quite amazing.

A Keith Richards look-alike and peacemaker at IORR, "Rockman" had his nickname of "Rocky" for a long time, when he was growing up in Australia. While he goes by other names too, Rocky turned into to "Rockman" because of his love of music, soul, blues, R and B, and most obviously, rock 'n roll, in particular because of the Stones. When asked about how he got his nick, Rockman reverted to his particular brand of Aussie humor, stating, "The captain gave it to me while I was on the chain-gang." He is well known on IORR for his jocular contributions to threads, for posting pics and articles from his massive archives on the Stones and other groups, and for helping members to calm down from heated, lengthy arguments. Sitting next to him at the O2 in London for one of the final shows of the ABB tour, I saw how a few people acted when recognizing him or when introduced. They would slowly greet him by name, saying in awe, as I did when I met him, "Rock-man?" Rockman dresses somewhat like his favorite Keith Richards, though a tad more formally in jackets, with his ubiquitous oblong scarves, his longish curly locks recalling earlier Stones eras. His avatar on IORR is a Keith photo from years back.

"Voodoo Chile in Wonderland" or Gerardo, co-leader of Rocks Off living in Mexico, liked the tune by Jimi Hendrix, "Voodoo Chile", pronounced almost as "child", he explains, not "chili", as some have called him. He likes the meaning of the name, "voodoo boy." He first named himself "Voodoo Lounge Chile" to mark the VL Stones tour as well as to honor Hendrix, soon subtracting the "Lounge" because people thought he meant a special food named for the 1990s tour, the hot bean soup Voodoo Lounge chili. Later he wrote that he added "in Wonderland" after Voodoo Chile "to make it more psychedelic. :)"

Real Names, Hometowns and States

Geography plus a first name determines some fans' choices. Cities or regions of the country are usually combined with mens' first names. "Detroit Ken" lives in the northern suburbs of that southern Michigan town. He describes how in spring, 2002, he started following Shidoobee right before the Stones *Licks* tour that started with rehearsals in Toronto. He needed a name to post online, and saw that

> the main local up there who was posting about the bands comings & goings as well as the songs being rehearsed was TorontoTom (he still posts) so i just picked my name from that, changing the city.

Also in Michigan, a guy named Jim used the state's abbreviation. He says he probably should have capitalized the MI instead of using "mi jim" because people think the handle is Mr. Jim or that the "mi" indicates "my" in Spanish. In "East Coast Steve Holmes'" case, he found out through the private list Undercover that a member there named Steve Holmes like himself lived out on the west coast, so he specified his region to avoid confusion. "Phillyrob" is easy to decode, city of birth in Pennsylvania plus first name, and likewise for Chicago_Dave from Illinois.

Females have geographical names too, but usually not combined with given names such as "Some Girl in Toronto," a name which is really a play on a song title, mixed in with a geographical reference. Another placed-based female is "TNVolsStonesfan" from Knoxville, Tennessee who is a "born n' raised Volunteer fan--football, basketball--we love it!" She joined her life long passion for the Stones to her allegiance to all her hometown college teams. From another state, and also a sports fan, named for the state mascot and teams, "Buckeyedave" loves the athletics at The Ohio State University. Another resident of Ohio, "ExiledinMedina" chose her name from her small city of 26,000 people located south of Cleveland and west of Akron, cleverly linked with the album title.

He doesn't have to claim he didn't inhale because he's never smoked a joint in his life, says "stonedintx." "The first part refers to the Stones", and he lived in Texas when he "joined the group," the Shidoobees, so he "just added them together." He thought "stonesintx" just didn't sound right, and "donintx," using his real name "Don" was "just plain boring." I met stonedintx in Las Vegas, standing in line when someone yelled out Shidoobee just to see if any of us from the online discussion board were around. We both answered and introduced ourselves.

"Mackie 212" describes how he took a shortened version of his last name and added the street he grew up on, "212th and Broadway in the Inwood section of Manhattan, NYC." He tells how in the early 70s when "graffiti was rampant" in the city, "it was a common practice to add your street to your nickname." He would occasionally get together with friends to do some spray painting to "mark up the old schoolyard."

An extremely affable gentleman with a grey beard, "Fred Hardin" likes when his brown hair is long so he can "feel like the real me", but wears it shorter at present. Fred is one of the few fans to use both his first and last names, similar to what many people do on Facebook, although a few will reveal them in their posts or in their emails. He explains, "On Shidoobee, I wanted people to know who I was when I met them." He adds that it is hard to keep up with all the screen names of different people there. On IORR, he now uses his full name in his signature, but he didn't feel as much "friendliness" in the environment, seeing more "nasty comments" posted regularly. For his official handle on IORR, Fred sticks to "Fred H," a shortened form of his real name, the moniker he chose when he signed up there. I met Fred in person in 2013 on the *50 and Counting* tour after getting to know him online for about seven years. At Shidoobee, he and I put forward the "It's not over!" mantra at intervals during the five years between *A Bigger Bang* and *50 and Counting*, countering strong voices who said, "It's over!" when the band going out again was in question.

Nicknames Bestowed by Others

"The Madame" was born after a group of women calling themselves the "cheetah sluuuts" for their love of animal prints decided one of their members should lead them. An early member Tongue Lady pronounced slut with an elongated "u" so they decided to spell it like that. They would call her "The Madame," inserting the defining article, transforming the plainer "Madame," indicating her place of leadership and honor in their ranks. A little older than the rest of them, The Madame could make sure the group took a decent picture together, "tummies in," smiling. That's when the idea came about to have a "number one" cheetah sluuut, The Madame. Members only needed an invitation from one of the group. When I had been around for a couple of years, honkytonkwom99 asked if I didn't think it was "about time" for me to join. She gave me a small leopard tongue pin, the emblem of the group, and someone sent me its match later on, in case I needed more. The Madame cites the criteria for admission is that a sluuut should be "a good person." These are "girls that like to have a good time," what we used to call the "good ol' broads." If one member approves of a possible candidate, her nomination translates to complete acceptance of the new person by the whole group.

The Madame remembers that her husband at the time "was totally horrified that such a name was given to me because he was a minister." The Madame's official username that accompanies every post is "GimmeLilDrink," a well-known line from the song "Loving Cup." Given The Madame's extremely moderate consumption of alcohol, the name truly calls for a "little" drink, or usually just for a diet pop or water. Her earlier user ID was "Gimme Flash," associated with her ex-husband Flash. When they divorced, she wanted a replacement and settled on "GimmeLilDrink," after it was suggested to her by Blue Lena. The cover band "The Glimmer Twins" dedicates their performance of "Loving Cup" to her when she is in their audience.

Art's nickname came from the Goodyear-type blimp, in this case, a zeppelin shape balloon in bright yellow, emblazoned with large red tongues and adorned with the Canadian and American flags near its tail. On May 7, 2002, it flew over The Bronx before dropping its cargo in a field in New York's Van Cortlandt Park. Out came The Rolling Stones, announcing their 2002-2003 *Licks* tour of North America, Europe, Asia and Australia, playing area, stadium, and theater shows. They performed a fifteen-minute set for the gathered group of credentialed journalists and photographers, with curious fans barricaded behind a fence.

A resident of Las Vegas, Art or "Artie" had talked to a Shidoobee fan who often organized events during tour stops there. She was coordinating her efforts with a friend of hers who had a web page dedicated to planning and announcements. Impressed by her friend's graphics that had borrowed the iconic image of this tour, the yellow blimp with the tongue emblem, she showed Artie the webpage. It was an animation of a dozen yellow blimps falling down the page from top to bottom. The fan said, "It looks like it's raining blimps! That's your board name!" Art said, "You're right," immediately warming to "Raining Blimps," recalling his nick of "Chevy" before that. He told me he wished he had saved the web page of moving tongues, that "she was so into it."

Others on Shidoobee referred to him by variations of the name, such as "Blimpies," "Blimpy," or as I called him, "RB." Attending his first Stones show in 1965, RB is no longer with us, dying unexpectedly at age 56 on June 11, 2011 after a short bout with a virulent brain cancer. His rapid illness and demise followed the death of his beloved brother Armand Joseph ("Papa Joe") Chevalier only nine days earlier. Friends from the Shidoobee board joined family members to celebrate him in a memorial held by his wife in Las Vegas on July 9, 2011. Art added his witty comments to Shidoobee almost daily, and to the real-time chat there that used to run every Friday night, reinstituted later on Saturdays.

You Get What You Need

His allegiance to the discussion board formed part of his obituary in *The Las Vegas Review-Journal*. People took advantage of his hospitable nature when visiting his place of residence in the desert, the gambling capitol of the U.S. The band played there every tour at least once and he was at all of those shows, once obtaining seats for the small concert at The Joint, holding 1000 seats. In the twenty- page prayer and memorial topic at Shiboodee dedicated to his brother, at first, and then to him, another fan said RB "missed his calling as a comedy writer," in the style of Dave Barry.

Art and I shared the bond of Ohio University, where I worked at its regional outpost, and where he was an undergrad on the main campus, and a noted Kiss fan at the time. I met him at the first art exhibit of Ron Wood's I attended in Las Vegas' Jack gallery at the Mandalay Bay hotel in November 2005. As he introduced himself, I saw how his baseball cap covered most of his brown hair just starting to gray, and how his large blue eyes shined, as he grinned.

Ronnie Wood inadvertently gave "Princess Margaret" her handle. On his tour with Bo Diddly, after the show she asked him to sign her copy of his solo album "1234": He asked her name and she told him Margaret, but, drawing from his English background, he signed it to "Princess Margaret." Margaret asks, "What else could I use?" The name complements her often quiet and dignified demeanor, befitting British royalty.

Another Rolling Stone served up very his own initials to one fan, with a twist. Not knowing all the details due to his reluctance to tell the full story, I have picked up from him and others only the bare bones. From what I understand, one fan met Keith Richards when he was very young, still in his teens. Meeting this slightly built fellow from England, Mr. Richards asked the young man's name when he agreed to sign a piece of memorabilia for him, and was told it was "Keith." Given Mr. Richards off-beat sense of humor, he wrote a note to "oldkr", causing the youthful

Keith to adopt the name in lower-case form as his online identity forevermore for his website and on the discussion boards.

My Own Nickname and Ending Thoughts on Online Names

As for me, "andee" was my online name since 1994, drawn from my childhood nickname "Andi," short for "Andrea." I changed the spelling after finding others had already used the original letters at online places. Many of my good friends and family have always called me andee, and now most of the people I'm friendly with online do too. I was densely unaware that most of the Shidoobees had Stones-related names, and on the other hand, I had not yet planned research and writing on the topic of online fans. When people wanted to know what my real name was, I could just say "andee", written on Shidoobee badges in both spaces for names, under online handle or "Shidoobee Name" and "Real Name." Leaders of boards other than Shidoobee, Bjornulf and Gazza of IORR and Rocks Off chose their real names or different versions of them for their handles. The leader of StonesVikings.com has a Stones-related name. I later discovered that all kinds of names existed at all of the boards, and that some posted on more than one, usually but not always under the same user ID. My nick at IORR and RO, joined after Shidoobee is "angee," a variation of "andee" and also fitting for a Stones fan, a play on the song title "Angie." It's a popular name for female fans," usually with numbers added to it, as in Angie541, to allow for adoption by multiple users.

I know the categories above are far from exhaustive. For example, a few people on Shidoobee and IORR go by job-related names, usually the professions or occupations that require specialized training. There is Mr. Lawyer, nursejane, dentist, and phd, to name a few, not to leave out DearDoctor, named for the song from *Beggar's Banquet*, not his job.

Of the four leaders of Shidoobee, IORR and Rocks Off, only Stonesdoug has a Stones nickname, as told above. The other three either use their own names, a variation of them, or a song from another artist. Observing over the last several years, and doing informal counts of people online during a given time of day, it seems to me that fans follow their leaders in that Shidoobees have a greater per cent of people with Stones-related names than the other two boards, with the smaller Rocks Off coming in second.

While Stones fans have all kinds of user names, I find especially intriguing how many fans work a feature of the band into their user id, often combined with their own names, characteristics, or locations. In an academic paper (2009), I have called this type of username a "blended identity," a mix of markers from personal life or individual preferences and an expression associated with an online group of like-minded fans, here, the fans of The Rolling Stones.

CHAPTER FOUR:

"BABY BREAK IT DOWN: HOW ONLINE COMMUNICATION ENRICHES THE STONES FAN EXPERIENCE"

"I wouldn't have gone to Paris if I wouldn't have met the people online." (Flairville)

With the Stones finding each other to form a band, and performing decades before the proliferation of personal computing and later on as well, their long-term fans have experiences that differ greatly during the pre-internet period and after the internet. The Word Wide Web (www) made print media less relevant as fans flocked to see who else shared their interests online. The author of *Under Their Thumb* (2008), a book about his days working with and for The Rolling Stones, Bill German stopped publishing his much-read fan newsletter *Beggar's Banquet* in 1996. He halted his hard-copy fanzine two years after the first browsers, Mosaic, and then Netscape allowed fans to easily connect worldwide, meeting in newsgroups and AOL. The major fan-run sites online began in the late 1990s and early 2000s, allowing fans to post text and pictures online so they could communicate about band members and their performances.

On a practical level, the internet has radically changed how people go about purchasing their tickets, how they find out about the best methods of procuring good seats, and how they can more easily trade and buy from each other after most of the tickets are already sold. As a by-product of these practices and also from a desire to share their love of the band, the fans have come to know other fans they would not likely have met by chance, even in their local areas. Without the internet fan boards, outside of friends they already know, the only fans concertgoers would meet and talk with are those sitting in their immediate vicinity or fans that would join them in line for tickets, merchandise or refreshments before or during the show.

A Computer-Mediated Proposal

Mixing the Stones and the internet fan group with an intimate personal moment, one fan got engaged at a Shidoobee party where his prospective bride was the only surprise guest. Joe Chavez came up with the idea through emailing friends from the online group. Other suggestions had him putting up a sign first outside and then inside on the bar's screen, and mooning her with writing on his behind. Instead, a cover band led by fans, the Zipmouth Angels were in on the act and ran a fake raffle. When Joe's girlfriend Connie's name was called, she came to the front expecting a grab bag of Rolling Stones paraphernalia, with stickers and CDs, and "the last thing she picked out was the ring." While this couple didn't meet on the fan board, and only Joe was a seriously hardcore Stones fan, he wanted to share one of the biggest moments in his life with the Shidoobees. Someone videotaped the event and disappeared from the group after that, but not before he made sure Joe got a copy. Oh, by the way, she answered, "Yes!" to his marriage proposal. They both still enjoy hanging out with the fans, flying in from Albuquerque to join the Shidoobees at Wildwood, New Jersey every year on Labor Day weekend.

How the Internet Increases Access to Theater or Club Shows

FenwayJoe speaks of how Shidoobee fans can help with the concert experience for travelers, for example, by telling others about the least expensive hotels and flights, how to negotiate public transportation, which neighborhoods to avoid, and where and when you can walk.

71

People know too whether you can wait to buy tickets or if it's best to purchase them ahead of time. In other words, having the board members is like having "several travel agents" at your personal disposal.

Theater shows of The Rolling Stones are rare events with small audiences, with "small" a relative quantity meaning less than 5,000 people or so. The first step in getting in is finding out when tickets are released. Little Queenie (LQ) of IORR notes that before the internet you had to find other means of procuring tickets, and knowing when they would go on sale. People would scour the newspapers or wait for tour and ticket sales announcements on the radio. With the internet, the site rollingstones.com posts the formal notices of show dates and provides links to ticket sales, timed differently for each city. Rumors as well as validated information fly across the internet, privately between fans and publicly on the fan group sites. Ebay becomes a source of tickets after the initial day of sale, and that was where LQ struck a deal with a seller for a small theater show at the start of the *Licks* tour in fall, 2002. She said she would save him a place in line where people queued up for the show outside the club if he would discount his price for her. When the show is general admission, the first people in line crowd toward the front, with Keith's side usually the preferable place to stand. Bartering with an ebay seller by trading a place in line for a ticket is an innovative strategy to get ahead in the audience game. She says "she sold herself" for that ticket to the Aragon theater show in Chicago. For those of us looking for any method possible of gaining entry to a theater show, LQ's tactics clearly worked. I tried by phone to get into that show, to no avail, before I had joined any of the online fan clubs, in their beginning years then.

Because of the huge fan base and the small capacity of the theaters, the tickets are sometimes released unexpectedly. The Aragon attended by LQ held 4500 in comparison to The Phoenix, a tiny club in Toronto that only seated 1000. After a rumored opening show there in Toronto, more like a final dress rehearsal before the *Bigger Bang* tour in 2005, people at Shidoobee put themselves on alert. One woman known as Stoneszone9 on the board was injured in an accident and decided to go anyway even though her friends said she belonged in a wheel chair. When she got the phone call that the time was right to leave, her female pal told her to be ready in twenty minutes. She got in the car with "a bottle of water," wearing her work outfit, "a skirt and blouse and a pair of heels and stockings." She would have to sleep out "on the street" in those clothes since she hadn't brought any other garments. After an eight-hour drive she stood in line for a chance at one of 250 tickets to be sold. People who knew her from Shidoobee would see her and ask, "What the fuck are you doing here?" knowing of her physical condition. Fans checked on her periodically during her wait through the night. They gave her a blanket and a pillow and one fan would periodically help her walk to the bathroom. She eventually scored a ticket. Her friend who ended up with a ticket bought by another friend took one look at her seated at a bar the next morning and said "You gotta go to bed." Stoneszone9 and the friend that drove them to Toronto from Philly ended up staying with a woman from out of town who posted on another online fan group, Undercover, whom they had never met f2f, but knew from reading her online.

Shidoobees who first met online did anything they could to help each other to go to the Beacon show filmed by Martin Scorsese for the documentary film *Shine a Light*. People tried any method that worked to get in, before the days of rehearsals and performances and during them. In my own case, desperate to attend the show, and on leave from work so I could go to New York that fall, I joined a "buying circle" on the group Undercover to procure a ticket, going cheaply then at 35 dollars. I could be online in the morning when the tickets went on sale. I enlisted the help of Peter Washkevich in Florida who couldn't go to the show, but who was willing to click links to increase the chances of finding me a ticket. Luckily his computer worked better than mine. While I was stuck at the alternate site for tickets, LiveNation, he procured a seat for me on Ticketmaster.

I had to trust him enough to give him my credit card number, not having met him in person and with no direct interaction online other than reading his occasional posts. In fan groups, especially a small one like Undercover, people have read each other online for years, and some have met each other face-to-face at shows or gatherings. The leader knows where we live, so to speak. Any violation of trust, any misconduct would rapidly spread around the group and beyond. I bought him a t-shirt in his size from the show, in gratitude, the black one with the Halloween symbols on it, the four tongues: an orange tongue with a Jack-o-lantern face, a light grey, mummified tongue, a green tongue with a spike through it and a scar on the lip, and the standard red tongue. They are collector's items now, each with the original date of the rescheduled show printed on the back, October 31, 2006.

International Traveling

The Stones typically run different "legs" of the tour, and timing, finances and work schedules allow different people to consider leaving their own countries and indeed, continents to travel to shows. Before I met the fans online it hadn't occurred to me to go to Europe just to attend a concert. The idea took hold of me and gathered steam. Why not go to England? Word was that the band was performing two nights (with a third added later) in a brand new venue in Greenwich, The Millennium Dome known as the O2, just outside of central London. One night, up late browsing for tidbits on IORR, the site with the most Europeans, as I dug around for information, I saw that someone had a single ticket for a first show to go with the one I had bought for the second show at the sale online. To see the boys in their own hometown at the very end of the tour, what an opportunity, I justified to myself. Not only that, I could talk to fans from all over the world. Finding the meeting place for the exchange of cash for ticket, I met a group of Stones fans at a posh hotel. Seated at the white-clothed table was a truly international group from Italy, Australia, Sweden, the UK and me, from the States. Among my four companions were the ticket-seller who had gathered us together, a person who didn't speak much English, an upper class divorcee, and a revered fan from the online community IORR. While in London I exchanged interviews with Philippe Puicouyoul who made a film interviewing fans about their feelings about The Rolling Stones, later shown at the Pompideau Center in his native France.

To procure seats closest to the stage, Rockman says he will use any means possible. He will "sleep out for tickets" and buy through other fans. A member of IORR, Rockman says that "a number of people have been wonderful in IORR in helping with tickets." Rockman has attended many concerts outside his home country of Australia, including the last few in London. Like many fans, he prefers Keith's side of the stage, (stage left), and usually gets it. He is popular with the IORR crowd, and is greeted with enthusiasm online and offline. When I met Rockman at the lunch in London to exchange my money for a decent floor seat, I was introduced to him unexpectedly, not knowing he would be there. My jaw dropped in surprise and happiness. He's made friends and close acquaintances through the internet who share rooms as well as ticket-buying strategies.

Rockman says that membership in IORR had a direct "influence on me going to the UK to see shows" and IORR posts give him a chance to see the layout of the concert sites to "memorize the EXIT points of the venue" before I arrive." Rockman typically mixes his more serious insights with humor, a trademark of his posts, especially in response to others who provide openings for jesting remarks.

Based in Northern Ireland, Gazza saw only European shows before he started up the website, Rocks Off (RO). His first American shows were in Hartford, Connecticut, 1999, and then he went to NYC in 2003 for the *Licks* tour. He saw the band in an arena, MSG, and in Giants stadium. Since the travel was so expensive, finding someone to stay with deferred some of the costs, such as the nights he spent with Sander in L.A. Of his forty-seven shows at the time of his interview before the last two tours, four were in the U.S., with the other forty-three in Western Europe and the UK. Gazza notes how people from all the sites, RO, IORR, and Shidoobee met in England for pre-parties on the *Bigger Bang* tour. Because the band played for three nights in one town, London, people could gather more easily, staying at the same hotel, and visiting the same bars through each show. He speaks of Shidoobees going out together frequently between shows, facilitated by how many of those fans reside in the Northeastern U.S. where the leaders live.

PartyDoll Meg became very good friends with a couple of people on RO and acquaintances with many more. She and Lady Jane who don't live in the same local area keep in contact regularly both by phone and by email. In the States the people she knows "all go to Tom's barbecue" in Louisville, KY. Even though she posts more on RO, she goes to parties arranged by members of both Shidoobee and RO. She started out slowly with her concert attendance, even though she had listened to the music all along. She bought tickets to a few shows on *Bridges to Babylon*, and a few more for *No Security* and then went " a little crazy" for *A Bigger Bang*. She usually had a friend from RO to go with her, but went to London alone, hanging out with Gazza, head of RO, from Northern Ireland. Meg felt okay about that because "he said 'he'd take care of me.'"

One of my U.S. respondents maintains that fans are friendlier in London than at home. After going there, I tend to agree that more people are open to talking about almost anything when meeting outside of the mainland U.S. There may just be a greater diversity of fans with wider interests, or when away from home, true for many fans in London, people may act more extroverted, more outgoing.

Making Friends and Having Fun

Describing social activities among fans, a woman named Thru and Thru tells how the parties are "almost as much fun as the concerts," calling the New York city festivities at Walter's bar "legendary". The man who got married at a Shidoobee function, Joe Chavez agrees that the people there are a main attraction during tours. During the *Licks* tour in Las Vegas, Thru and Thru had "so much fun" going to the Betty Boop bar with fans after the show, staying out long enough to make the early breakfast. The well-oiled fans caused a ruckus in the restaurant and "everybody was shushing us," says Thru and Thru, though "Doug kept saying, 'I just want an egg.'" She made it back to her hotel about 7:00 a.m. to meet her husband who asked, "Where the hell have you been?" Many of these revelers were well past their forties.

Joining Thru and Thru for pre-parties at Walter's near where he lives is common for Shidoobee Yesterday's Papers. While he says he's "not a good mixer," failing to "insert myself into the conversation", he did attend a pre-party in Chicago where he recognized someone. It was Voodoopug, a large man, hard to miss, according to Yesterday's Papers who introduced himself to him and to another fan and "the evening just flowed."

Thru and Thru comments that reading the boards lets you "get caught in the hype" so that you want to attend more concerts. You read "who's going to which concerts…who's going to be there," and that makes you want to go. I have found that true, that reading the fan discussions whets my taste for more and more shows. The enthusiasm for any show plants the idea to consider if it's possible to go, thus carrying a fan further along in the process of actually attending.

She signed up for Rocks Off because they had all the set lists of the European shows. Thru and Thru said that Shidoobee "turned her off" when they dropped interest in the tour during the second European leg of *ABB*, whereas IORR "can't be beat" for information when the Stones play in Europe. She was born in Germany and visits Europe when she can. Even so, she doesn't post much on IORR, and concludes that "RO is "a little bit too wild and crazy" for her, that's she's too old for it. Thrillingly, T and T made the cut after tryouts for the introductory fan film on *50 and Counting*.

GAFF describes his delight at interacting with people from the fan board:

> *For me it's so fun to get to know people on the board, and then meet them at the show, hugging and kissing them like you've known them all your life, I've never been one to get into chatrooms, I'm not a social butterfly on the internet, I never go to myspace. Shidoobee is a very unique place."*

He always goes to the pre-parties and called Stonesdoug "a minor celebrity," who has met everyone on the board. GAFF concurs that his participation in Shidoobee has affected the number of Stones shows he attends: "My Stones exposure's gone through the roof because of Shidoobee." My own concert attendance soared from two or three per tour to seven on *A Bigger Bang* with two in another country, and then five shows in the U. S. during the nine months of *50 and Counting*. Of course I had started the research during the ABB tour, which didn't hurt, but my enthusiasm came from reading the boards.

Often attending far-away shows with people from the board, at the LA forum concert, GAFF took a picture of a fan standing near the stage when she tossed up a blue Shidoobee bracelet caught and worn by Ronnie for the rest of the show. The photo is very dear to the female fan and also to all the Shidoobees as evidence of a Rolling Stone recognizing and valuing the fan group. Ronnie wore one of the bracelets at points along the tour. I had two from the limited quantity sold at Shidoobee, and wore them thereafter to concerts, until I misplaced one, treasuring the remaining blue bracelet. I know Ronnie recognizes the bracelets in the audience and I have the sense that other Rolling Stones do too.

Hearing that "people were following them around like The Dead," Glenn, also known as durtysox points to his heads-up light-bulb moment from paying attention to a Shidoobee member who did just that. He thought, "I could be doing that the whole time," and his concert attendance skyrocketed. It was when durtysox met Stonesdoug that he thought, "Wow, these other people went from city to city." When asked how membership in Shidoobee may have affected his concert attendance, Glenn said he didn't even consider traveling to shows before he got to know the leader of Shidoobee. His number of shows almost tripled after he came onto the Shidoobee board, rising from four to eleven on the next tour.

In the early days before Shidoobee replaced aol.com, durtysox supplied the karaoke parties with his P. A. system. Much later, after he "made friends with this guard," he hung out outside the Beacon with other Shidoobees in the area, including kingbee and two others. They had gathered to listen to the rehearsals of band during the week before the filming of the concerts for Scorsese's film *Shine a Light*.

Flairville either goes to concerts with his girlfriend, now wife, who is not fond of the band, or with friends from the boards. He said he would never have gone to Paris if not for the info and the people on IORR. As an Englishman in Paris, "it's a bit hard" to meet people, "at first" and "then you feel like you've always been there." He went to Paris on his own, and "met all these people" in bars and hotels. They "went to gigs together," were at "the gold circle standing on the pitch." "We all went in together and did the same things." Without knowing people from IORR "I wouldn't have gone to Paris," he says.

Starting

Starting a club by mail and phone after the "Stockholm trilogy" of Stones concerts, Mickijaggeroo and his pals from Sweden and other cities nearby limited the number of members to twenty-one. "We are an elitist club," says Mickijaggeroo. The original nine joining are the board of the group, which now has its own website, stonesvikings.com. The site contains detailed profiles of all the members, only one of whom is female, along with links to individual band member's' sites and other fan communities devoted to the Stones. They wear specially designed black t-shirts, each with a Stones tongue adorned with the horns of a traditional Viking helmet.

Members of Stonesvikings traveled independently to the U.S. and throughout Europe from Sweden on the last tour. But, once in the gig towns "we try as far as possible to stay at the same hotel, and always hang out together," explains Mickijaggeroo. They get tickets in smaller groups unless they are able to find enough tickets in a row for all of them. They "always party together" before and after the shows and always travel together when within the city of the show.

The members get together from time to time to "socialize outside the Stones community." "If somebody is feeling depressed" or going through a divorce, the group joins to support its members.

> *When there's no tour we try and visit each other privately. I just got home from one of the Vikings yesterday where we stayed four Vikings together over Easter, and had some fun listening to Stones, having beers, etcetera.*

If they wouldn't have decided not to expand, the group "could be 3000 today." They wanted to keep it small so that the close ties would prevail. The club's president values the communication and emotional bonding of people or friendship much more highly than collecting numbers of fans. While people from other fan groups come together sometimes outside of concerts to interact in pairs and larger groups, this small club explicitly encourages strong friendships among its membership.

Commenting how the internet makes it possible for worldwide communication, Pauline cites the friends she has made as the best result of being online. Online communication has also helped her with the business she has started of booking backing musicians for concerts close to her home base of Amsterdam. People from the fan groups at IORR and RO, and from the musicians from her Stones network brought it to life full-blown when the Stones began their tour in Europe.

Pauline only started seeing the band in the late 1990's, but she thought the experience should be shared with others:

Mind you, my first live show was 1998, rather late! I had always wanted to go to their gigs, but nobody ever wanted to join me.

Now I get to meet the same group of fans from all over the globe. I pick up my tickets from the Stones hotel, meet with the guys who play with the Stones. After the show I rush out and have a beer with the guys. If the Stones tour in Europe, I try to see as many shows as I can. Hence we drive to Dusseldorf from Amsterdam, share the same car, play Stones music, have a laugh, book a hotel...

Meeting Stones fan online has brought her early dreams of seeing the band live into practice, and more, as she travels the area with like-minded folks. Pauline says "I've gotten to know some very dear friends from all over the world and I am very grateful for that," crediting the internet for making that possible.

How people come to feel as if they know each other, and can even share rooms with folks they've never met has to do with expression of self, first through username and avatar. A person presents facets of himself or herself, in this case through the choice of a user id, in the case of the

Shattered board, usually related to the Stones. Creativity comes into play as well as familiarity with song titles, album names, and lyrics. The pictorial image selected as an avatar can also provide clues to the type of person posting. The posts themselves of course contain hints on the sense of humor of the fan, the scope and depth of interest in the band and the music, and how the person interacts with others on the board.

Two Cases of Housing Arrangements

Very early in my Shattered membership someone offered to share a room in Las Vegas at the MGM Grand where the Stones were playing. Even though the fan was a complete stranger and male, I had little hesitation in taking him up on his offer. The room itself was more than I could afford alone and I hardly saw the guy all weekend. His wife actually wrote from her home to tell me he was there but hadn't checked in yet. Okay, there was an awkward moment or two. The background fact is that I could check with other people about him before the interaction and see other posts he had made over the weeks and months. I knew that he was risking his reputation (as was I) with the community if anything untoward happened.

Later on, a male fan invited a female to stay with him in his apartment in an area near the concert venue. He didn't make advances toward her, though he did become extremely upset when something minor went wrong, a technical household glitch that occurred during the visit. The man yelled for a long time and his guest insisted on going back to the airport, leaving earlier than was planned. He drove erratically to the airport, in his anger, scaring the female fan, and was asked to leave the board soon after the incident. I had made tentative plans to stay with him and attend a concert too, and luckily, he didn't follow up with me.

Online/Offline: Connections, Information, and Set Lists

For some fans their early use of the internet was tied to The Rolling Stones. They got online and set about finding out information about the band and the concerts. Their search often led them to the fan boards, once those were started, when they Googled the Stones. Occupied with other projects, I didn't come upon these fan groups until just before the start of *ABB*. I read them for almost two years before I began the project of writing about the fans. I either went with a friend or alone to concerts in the previous ten years before joining or with my brother to shows in Chicago. Not only has my concert attendance increased since joining the online fan groups, but also socializing with others before the shows quickly became routine.

What's nice is getting to know people online to the extent that you really feel you have a sense of what they're like before meeting them in person. After reading public posts, you can follow up a feeling of connection with any individual in private messaging or email. Anyone can come to a gathering and feel welcomed by at least some of the other members, those who are sensitive to newcomers. One guy told me he especially pays attention to new fans from outside the geographical area of the fan meeting, making newcomers feel at home very quickly. Shidoobee instituted the tradition of the "Virgin" ceremony, to initiate people new to the yearly celebration in Wildwood, New Jersey. The recorded or live music you hear in the background is pleasing to people there. It's almost always by The Rolling Stones. Locals contact commercial bars near venues of concerts requesting they play the music for the evening. for pre-show gatherings. No one asks to change it to something else. People have formed relationships ranging from casual acquaintances to good friendships to dating to occasional marriages resulting from the mix of offline and online contacts.

Online the wealth of information on any topic is astounding. A fan has only to ask a question about, for example, who played on an obscure song, or the identity of someone in a photo with a band member, and others jump into answer or to puzzle out leads to the solution. To know that you can go online any time of the day or night to see people who share your passion for the band makes you feel part of a community, even when the band is not touring. These hard core fans wear Stones clothing, collect Stones books, and try to go to any show they can. Except for the very tightest of ticket situations, fans in the online groups are selling extras that they bought and don't need anymore because of their own upgrading to better seats, or because a friend dropped out. Normally, the ethics in the online communities forbid selling them there for a profit to keep prices reasonable. As noted, in the middle of the night, I once found a good seat for a show in London, picking the ticket up from the seller. Buyers and seller met at a London hotel, where we all dined together, several fans, each from a different country.

Fans have an endless fascination with the set lists of each concert, whether they attend or not. On its home page IORR has listings of all years of a tour from 1994, when Bjornulf started collecting the information online. The years link first to all the concert venues and cities, and then to the set lists for each show during every month of the tour. Several reviews of each show are posted after each set list, beginning consistently in 2002. At Shidoobee, each show has its own thread, and the set list is posted in it as soon as it becomes available. During each show, someone in the audience calls or texts a community member, who then posts the set list song by song. Much excitement ensues on the real time chats as each song is announced, particularly at the beginning of a tour, and when unexpected changes occur in the songs or even their order. Particularly at IORR, people try to post videos of tunes from ongoing shows as soon as they can, if they are there and taping.

Stonesdoug sets up individual show topics when the tours and concert venues are announced. Shidoobee contains the tours from the start of its existence in 2000. The topics detailing the set lists begin with the 2002 *Licks* tour. The Shidoobees attending a particular concert sign in and Doug composes a list of all members going to each show. In the archived threads, the post of the attendees follows the set list and precedes the reviews. During the first tour covered by Shidoobee,

84

people announced the location of their seats along with their attendance so others could find them at the venue, but this practice largely stopped, most likely replaced by private messaging or email between fans.

In the original tour threads on Shidoobee, IORR and RO when the shows are ongoing, more information pops up on each show such as how much success people have with Ticketmaster with or without a Rolling Stones.com fan club membership, of late no longer in existence. The Rolling Stones fan site had charged $100.00 a year to institute a "legacy platinum" track that allowed for early access to tickets. Whether those seats were much better than later rounds of tickets released is much debated on the boards. At one point, before *ABB*, members could regularly score cheap seats for the first 10 rows.

Once the tour starts, people pour over the set lists, looking for their length to check how many songs are played at each show, finding out if there are changes in the song choices or not, and exactly where and what they are, if so. Some withdraw from the debate, saying they are just happy the band is playing. Fenway Joe says, for him, "It's not a biggie at all...I'm not one of these set list junkies...if they don't play certain songs, they're going to jump off the bridge." He also says there are songs that he's never heard played and that "it would be nice to hear them sometimes." Certain fans celebrate each time a more unusual song is played, both at the show and online. At a show in Columbus that I attended, the song "Sway" was played for the first time at a concert, with Mick's introduction: "We're gonna do this one that we've never done before." In the audience, a smattering of people screamed and clapped. People commented on the boards afterwards that the hardcore fans loved it, but others in the audience seemed bewildered during the song, not recognizing it. The *Licks* tour of 2002-2003 in particular had a varied set list. Keith nicknamed it the "Fruit of the Loom" tour at the Stones press conference, for the different sized venues they would play, small, medium, and large.

Representing many who appreciate but don't require variety, Blue Lena points out that shows vary in quality, regardless of the set list:

Obviously, having attended so many shows it's nice to have some rarities in a set list... It was not always the set list that made the show. I mean, I may have seen a spectacular show with all warhorses, or a so-so show with rarities, but certainly new or rare songs in a set make a show more special for diehards like me.

She calls people who constantly complain about the songs played "set list whiners," a term adopted by online fans who prefer to leave the issue alone. I am in her camp, though I like to pore over the posted series of songs played as a prelude to attending shows. I have run into people who would much rather be surprised by the songs included and their order, the way they were before the flow of internet information.

The larger the venue, the more standard the set lists, on the whole. During the *Bigger Bang* tour, a person on Shidoobee posted a chart tracing every song in the tour and how much it was played at each show, studied in detail by fans, as each show took place. Well over half the set list stayed the same, the warhorses, while their spot in the set list could shift. Toward the end of the tour, the same four or five songs always finished the set list, in the prescribed order. When the opening song changed at rare times, the hardcore fans were primed for a special concert. At the Columbus, Ohio show in 2005, I was thrilled to hear the opening notes of "Brown Sugar" to start the show.

A list of these frequencies for various tours and even for all live shows appears occasionally at IORR though not in graphic form at first. Many fans posts questions about when and where a tune was played live or recorded. Considering the large body of songs Jagger and Richards have written and recorded, and how many songs the band has covered (see keno.org/songlistnlyrics.htm), the desire of the hardcore fan is to have the Stones dig deeper into its catalogue.

Word has it that the current keyboard player Chuck Leavell influences the set list by talking it over with Mick, suggesting a few tunes that have not been played much. Even Keith Richards who may be open to a greater variety than Mick has said that if the singer can't sing it, we can't play the song. Fans believe that people from the Stones camp read the fan boards and see which songs the fans propose. There was a brouhaha one tour when the fans supposedly voted on the internet for a certain song. When "Ruby Tuesday" was played, they protested that they had voted differently, and that the poll results were fixed. When guest artists supposedly played winning songs on *50 and Counting,* hardcore fan skepticism on the legitimacy of the voting rose even higher.

Another closely watched number is how many songs are played at each show. Serious fans protest when the set list length is cut, which usually shortens the concert. Carl the Lobsterman, the son of a lobster fisherman from Maine puts it this way:

My only complaint is give me two hours and five minutes…Don't start a tour with 23 songs and take it back to 19…I don't buy that you have to cut the show back…In '89 they played for two hours and twenty minutes. Just don't have the people pay the same freight in California for 19 songs that people in Boston pay for 23 songs…Shidoobees in New York deserve 23 songs.

The band has lately started a tour with more songs than it plays later on, a practice not noticed by casual fans.

Some fans track the whereabouts of the band from when they hit a city to when the show is over and afterwards. One person on Shidoobee with access to local flight diagrams was able to tell when their plane was due in and when it had flown and landed. A few protested that this posting had given too much information to fans online, a case of TMI that possibly bordered on stalking. Others try to stay at the Stones hotels in hopes of catching glimpses of the band members, or they hang out there at the bars. These places are regularly noted at the various online fan groups, or at least shared between individuals who are friends. Expenses can prevent people from staying at the top hotels, depending on the city. I gave a thought to booking a room at the band's hotel off the beach of Rio de Janeiro for their free concert drawing 400,00 in February 2006, but I gave up the idea when I decided I couldn't take off work to travel to South America. I had an online friend there who would have provided me a free place to stay, the reason I originally entertained going. Often the backup band comes into the hotel bars to drink after the shows, and in some towns, the Stones may drop in briefly, or for longer periods, especially if they are playing more than one show in the area. In Europe, especially, where security seems looser than in the U.S., throngs of fans commonly wait outside the hotel for glimpses and sometimes even the chance of a signature on an album, poster, or piece of apparel. They are often rewarded with signings.

In the U.S., before the two Beacon theater shows filmed for a movie, fans in Midtown Manhattan stood as close to the stage door as they could, where the Stones waved upon arrival but didn't sign autographs because of security limiting crowds to the other side of the street. For rehearsals, during a chilly, rainy week in October, a few local residents waited near the venue for the principles to enter and exit, hoping for a wave, a signature or even a brief hello. One person reported on her initial lack of success for the first days, although another person outside posted that he heard several songs rehearsed on the Thursday before the first scheduled show.

When the second Beacon show was postponed, word spread quickly online that fans that had seats would have to wait another day to attend. Glencar attended the Wednesday rehearsals and said online the next day at Shidoobee:

They did "Connection" twice & "Some Girls" twice. I also heard "Ain't too Proud" to beg. The big guard at the stage door chased me away, but a nice girl around back let us stand by the door for a while. The guy who was there for the closed rehearsal wouldn't let me stand there. (Closed rehearsal-meaning no camera or crew in the room.) The second rehearsal, after their dinner, started around 7:45 and was for the cameras to rehearse as well. You could only really hear if you had your ear about an inch from the crack in the door. (NY streets are noisy, plus there are tractor-trailer generators running.) It was cool hanging out, but I don't think I'm going to bother with it today.

Often the band plays rarer cuts in rehearsal than they do in concert. In this case, the band did play an infrequent but not unheard of song "Some Girls," and "Connection," a tune almost never heard, possibly requested by Martin Scorsese, the director of the filmed concert. In the film, Scorsese showed a hand-written set list that seemed to come out of his personal favorites, with columns for rarely played and never played.

After the shows people come online to review not only the technical details of the performances, but also the character of the venue and the audience, often contextualizing their experience in comparison to other shows of the tour or other shows in their lifetime of concert-going. Fans chime in to challenge or support each other's perceptions. If the show is unusual, discussion can go on for weeks or even months afterwards. Photos and even videos appear to enhance the online experience for people unable to attend.

The internet has greatly added to the fan's experience of The Rolling Stones. An IORR member posted recently:

Look how the internet has changed our knowledge of The Stones. Years ago we found out that The Stones were coming to our town by the local newspaper or an announcement on the local

89

rock radio station. We didn't know what city they played before or where they were going next. We now know every show they ever played. Every set list. We even find out what songs are being played in another city before the show is finished. We bought tickets in ONE location. First in line guaranteed you first row. Now we can buy tickets from our PC for a show 2000 miles away.

Whatever nostalgia remains for the old days before the internet, most fans greatly appreciate the convenience of online buying and communicating, features of everyday life that mainly enhance the concert experience. Meeting fans from online and then encountering them at shows and gatherings has led to more enjoyment and sharing of the fandom as well as new local and long distance friendships that wouldn't have happened without the online forums.

CHAPTER FIVE:

"CAN YOU HEAR THE MUSIC: GOING TO LIVE SHOWS FROM THE EARLY DAYS THROUGH *A BIGGER BANG* TOUR"

"You know there was a time you didn't need pit tickets, just determination." (ugotthesilver)

The peak experience for a music fan is to see a live show. Before a tour announcement, fans gather in excitement online, the topics multiply, and people not seen in years emerge to give an opinion or ask a question. Who knows what? Which information is accurate, which is likely false? Prior to the internet, people found out about shows through other media. Local radio stations and newspapers provided clues on upcoming shows and dates of ticket sales and word of mouth spread both the rumors and facts.

Chronology and Themes

This series of vignettes from fans takes us through the early days of Stones to the close of *A Bigger Bang* Tour in 2007. I divide the touring period into large swatches of time, or stages beginning with Part I, the sixties and seventies into the early '80s, from 1962-1981, followed by their next group of tours, Part II, in the later eighties and nineties from 1989 through 1999, and then finally, Part III, the tours of the early 21st century, from 2002-2007.

Because I drew almost exclusively from fans in online communities, I have missed many who went to the first series of concerts, people in their teens or twenties back in the early sixties, a relatively small pool of people among all Rolling Stones fans. The older fans heard them at first on the radio or television the in sixties, and some were lucky enough to see shows early on. I've divided the concert experiences into groups based more upon fan attendance at tours than attempting to mark historical periods of the Stones by when a band member left, for example. I let both the start dates of the large American and European tours and the experience of my interviewees determine the divisions. Thus, the first period goes from the beginning through 1981, covering almost the first twenty years of history of the band, including their first British tour in 1963 and ending with their last tour of that era. The second period begins in1989 when they started up again after a seven-year absence from the road, spanning four major tours through 1999, and the third and last period goes from 2002 forward, running through two tours, ending in August 2007, and then shows after that.

Performances for their fiftieth anniversary comprise the tail end of the third era, a group of selective dates in 2012 and 2013, signaling perhaps the beginning of the finale for the band. The special "pit" experiences of fans at their fiftieth anniversary shows of 2012 and 2013 are described in the next chapter. The 2014 dates, largely beyond the scope of this book, and brief thoughts about what may come in 2015 and beyond are touched on in the final pages, the epilogue.

Before describing aspects of the concerts through the eyes of the fans, I will frame these experiences by looking at the two songwriters, Mick and Keith. Understanding that some fans appreciate Charlie or Ronnie the most, with others harkening back to Brian Jones and the days of bass player Bill Wyman, Mick and Keith provoke most of the fan gaze at shows and attention in media coverage. Following fan characterizations of Mick and Keith, each time period evokes certain themes, with sex and drugs most prominent in Part I, along with conflicts with relatives and friends about going to shows. Part II begins with fan comments on waiting for the band to return until band members ended their long hiatus, and contains stories of problems among fans at shows or between fans and security personnel. Another thread in Part II is how fans from far-flung neighborhoods, cities and countries came to know each other, getting together for shows. In the years before the World Wide Web, fans began to meet at venues and through offline publications run by people including Bjornulf Vik and Bill German. After that, many became acquainted in online fan groups. Part III brings the whole experience of going to shows to life by centering on individual fans at club shows or other special events, as they happened. Fans talk about facets of the concert-going process from getting tickets or passes, to waiting in line, to reactions to what they saw and heard.

Mick or Keith: Favorite Rolling Stone

When people go to shows, they may watch the whole band, and then often concentrate on one player. Nursejane stood next to me close-up at a show, looking at Keith the whole time, even while Mick engaged in all of his showmanship. She always has to be on "Keith's side" of the stage on the right side of the audience (at stage left), though Keith moves about quite a lot these days. Ronnie fans want to go to the left side of the crowd (at stage right), "Ronnie's side," usually an easier spot to score because fewer fans are dedicated to getting there. With his outgoing personality, Ronnie interacts with the crowd more than the rest of the band does. Charlie is a favorite of some, though he is harder to watch, located at the back of the stage, blocked by the other band members or not in immediate view of the audience. Shyer than the others offstage, he prefers to stay personally unengaged with anyone outside the band onstage, on the whole, while tossing out his sticks into the crowd at the end of the show. Mick is all over the place, with his microphone just left of center these days, so Mick fans will sit anywhere, unless they love Keith too and shoot for Keith's side. Just to note, the few fans in this project who have seen Brian Jones represent a much larger audience who continue to talk about him, and would choose him as their favorite if he would have lived.

Most fans choose Mick or Keith as their favorite. What fans want from each band member is eye contact, a glance of recognition. Keith may play a good chunk of a song for you, giving attention directly through his music, and throwing out the occasional guitar pick, often targeted toward a devotee. Some fans point to Mick's aloofness, but for females, especially, he can share a section of a song, maintaining eye contact while he dances, if he is not worried about a particular passage. Both recognize individual fans, nodding and smiling. Mick will give a wave or blow a kiss in between song phrases. These gestures from the band are rewards to those who secure a place close to the stage.

Mick and Keith are each described differently by fans and writers, as if they are polar opposites. Mick is seen as the "head," more rational and less emotional, vs. Keith's seen as the "heart" of the band, the soulful one. Mick is the performer, the actor, the front man who will appear outwardly to give everything he's got, in movement and voice. He usually does, "leaving it all on the stage," for the good of the show. Keith is portrayed as the more genuinely demonstrative guy, more himself onstage, the warmer persona, though often called "cool" in slang terms. Beneath his rough exterior, fans see depth of feeling in Keith, a sincerity, whereas Mick's charms appear more on the surface, even as they both age. Rather than a womanizer, some see Keith as a true lover of women, monogamously inclined. While a rebel, a non-conformist in many respects, in his own self-description he is happiest when settled down with one female at a time, now partnered with Patti Hansen for over three decades. Mick clearly enjoys female company, with a history of two spouses and a few long-lasting live-in relationships. In contrast to Keith, however, he has demonstrated that he has no intention of staying completely faithful to any one partner, proclaiming recently that marriage does not work for him.

Ironically, with all the combustibility, they probably have much in common, both serious musicians who wrote all those songs in their Jagger-Richards collaboration, originally bonded by a love of American blues along with geographical origins in the London area. They even named themselves the "Glimmer Twins" back in the 1960s. They share an offbeat, self-deprecating humor, and lately, chuckle together during moments onstage. Each seems to relish his time with his children, now mostly adults, some with their own kids who are the duo's grandchildren, and Mick's great-grandchild born in 2014. They are both fire signs, Keith the Leo and Mick the Sagittarius, for what that's worth, highly compatible in the astrological world.

Although both have plenty of fans from both genders, men are more apt to proclaim their devotion to Keith, while more women than men openly praise Mick. Online, some of Mick's female admirers call themselves "Mick chicks," while Keith fans are either female "Keith babes" or male "Keithoholics." Men and women who play the guitar analyze Keith's technique, naming him "the riffmaster" or "the human riff." Mick is appreciated for his vocals and phrasing, his moves, and charisma. Male and female fans express "love" for each member and the whole band, meaning everything from a personal attraction to most universally, a deep appreciation for the music and performance, as outlined in Mark Duffett's discussion of "fan words" (*Popular Music Fandom*, 2014).

Among the Keithoholics at Shidoobee, crossfire hurricane describes his ongoing appreciation of him, how he was "always Keith" when the Stones music came on and at live shows:

I'd be jamming my air guitar and doing my best Keith impersonation. It is an impersonation that I still do at every Stones show without even realizing it. My son busted my chops about it after seeing me doing it when I brought him to his first show in 2005.

Crossfire calls Keith "the essence of cool," saying if he could have become a rock star, he would have "modeled" himself after him.

He has a unique way of commanding attention while remaining laid back. He's created some of the most incredible music ever recorded while managing to look like a bad ass at the same time. Plus it's very obvious that he's having a great time doing it....

He has a way of carrying himself that makes me think; Damn how friggin cool would it be to hang with Keith for a night.

Likening singling out Keith to how we choose our friends, crossfire notes that friends are picked for certain qualities they have that "make your life just a little better when you're with them." He knows he's joining many others who feel the same who gather to talk about Keith online and offline.

BlindMellon has changed his focus from Charlie at the beginning to Mick and then to Keith. At first he studied Charlie because he wanted to play the drums like him. Then he switched to Mick because of his domination in the media through pictures and interviews, and his "unique vocals." More recently, he admires Keith more and more for "his playing, coolness, and his desire to keep playing" despite any obstacles. He notes that for shows, Keith wants to "take risks by trying out different songs," whereas Mick seeks perfection, wanting "the safety and security of playing what he knows best." In debates on content of the set lists at shows, Mick has said that most audience members don't react to new or unfamiliar songs from the past, becoming bored after the first notes. He knows the small number of diehards relish the rarities.

Female fans devoted to Keith point to how much more "approachable" he is than Mick, and how pleasurable it is "to see him smiling all the time." One who has grown to like Keith over the years says

You Get What You Need

I have to admit Keith is now my favorite. Mick's cool, but Keith is real...He' spontaneous, doing his thing because he loves to play, having fun, not a worry in the world. He gets in the zone...

One Mick chick says that while "it's ALWAYS been Mick," she has also come to appreciate Keith after experiencing the Stones live. Watching him onstage she says that Keith "has burrowed into my heart and there he will stay." She hadn't realized before that "under that gruff exterior lives a sweet, funny, soulful man."

On the other hand, a male fan chooses Mick because he is a bit of a "contrarian," knowing Keith is the choice of many on Shidoobee and IORR. He feels Mick contributes to the band as songwriter as well as onstage. He always thought, as a lyricist, Mick "was underappreciated." In performance, Mick is "incredible," and "the defining front man of rock and roll." He says Keith fans want to believe that Keith is "the grit of the band," but they seem to forget that Keith was the main writer of the ballad "Angie," a tender ode to a girlfriend, to what might have been.

Another man with a passion for sports points to Mick because of his unique persona.

Lou Gehrig was a GREAT, GREAT, GREAT baseball player but you'd never know he was around when Babe Ruth was in the room...Same thing with Mick. He's truly one of a kind.

A man says he relates most to Mick because he loves to sing and play harmonica. He finds Mick's songwriting amazing and wants "to be Mick Jagger" when he grows up. Nonetheless, he finds Ronnie the one he would most want to hang out with offstage.

A female goes for Mick in particular, onstage:

I love all the band members of course, great individuals, but must confess I can count on one hand the number of times I've

97

*taken my eyes off MICK during a performance! :eek The
ultimate frontman, then, now and forever, who will definitely go
down in Rock & Roll history!*

She joins another female who claims the name "Mick Jagger" will be
recognized more than the other band members in the "decades
(centuries?) to come." Another female says Mick is "the face" of The
Rolling Stones, immediately recognizable. She concludes that "even
people who don't follow the music will know of Mick Jagger."

From the Netherlands, Calista Wissing hadn't become aware of The
Stones until 1995 when she went with a large group of people just to
"experience a big concert." At the time before her first show, she didn't
know who all the Stones were. She and her husband were in the middle
of the field, and she remembers when the band came on at eight or nine
o'clock, she asked him, "Is that Mick Jagger?" And he said "No, Keith
Richards." Calista's reaction to first seeing Mick onstage was:

*Mick jagger in a red coat walked towards the piano. It was love
at first sight, that feeling, amazing what a sight, like a
magnetism. I think that happened a lot, not only the person of
Mick Jagger fascinated me, this man dressed in red sitting at the
piano...*

*What happened on that night, I think that the Stones and
especially Mick Jagger, made it possible for me to feel myself
more free. I was brought up very protected, a good person that
always keeps accounts for others, and is living according to
certain rules, very neat, a good girl... sociable. The Stones
confronted me with another spectrum, more the dark side of
human beings... It was liberating for me.*

Calista had broken free from her old shackles of conventionality. The
counterculture era long gone, the vestiges of its spirit resided in the
band and its music that signaled a new set of possibilities.

You Get What You Need

The same year they went to Rotterdam, for her second show, and Calista's husband Robin went again the next night without her while she sat home alone. She had a "terrible evening," and since then has gone with him every time. In the 90s she went to almost every concert in Holland, but for the small Paradiso club show, she didn't get in. Calista made her banner "You Make a Grown Girl Cry," a play on the lyrics from "Start Me Up." She first held it up in 1998, but band members didn't really recognize it until 2003. Her fandom resulted in her taking a leadership role in Holland's Forty Licks Fan Club, running its website. I had the pleasure of meeting this articulate, charming brunette in person at a fan event in Belgium.

In São Paulo, Brazil, Gaby had to wait for over three decades after she began to like the band for them to come to South America. Just before they did, she saw a show in Miami, in December 1994. She was 44 in 1994, and had been a fan since she was fourteen. Her friends in Florida had bought tickets and mailed her a black spikey tongue t-shirt before the show. She sat up in "the nosebleeding seats with an obstructed view for the B-stage."

When the band announced they were coming to her area a month later, she said to herself, "I don't believe them this time." Gaby had friends living there with her. She bought the tickets, and someone made her a t-shirt from that tour. She "recorded everything from MTV," all that she could.

> It was the first show ever in South America. I thought it was a dream...I went with my daughter. She was 18 at the time. I was worried that I couldn't go to the front...She had lots of practice, and said, "Don't worry, I will take you to the front. We were at the third row.

Then the girl in front of her wasn't feeling well, so she could get a little further up, almost in the first row.

I felt I had eye contact with Mick. During "Start Me Up", my daughter saw it and pushed me closer. I was looking at him all the time, of course... for a fraction of a second...Mick's eyes and mine met.

Then it started "raining buckets." Gaby was soaking wet, but the band didn't stop though it poured through the whole show. At one point, Keith looked up at the sky and said, "Thank you," very "ironically," recalls Gaby.

Both Mick and Keith can stir up fans' initial feelings when they appear onstage on the sets. A man named Jumping Jack after the song who claims allegiance to the band since the start, JJ had to wait until 1975 to see his first shows, one with the unfolding lotus stage that raised and lowered. The first Buffalo concert in June had the flat lotus stage. For his entrance, "Keith started out with 'Honky Talk Women', looking around for Mick. He pops up through the door. That made quite a lasting impression." In all the years since, JJ still likes the lotus stage the best.

Very much a Mick chick, following his every move in performance, I also relate to Keith and his musical artistry, and to his facial expressions and onstage antics. I recall when Keith smoked a cigarette onstage in London, smiling broadly, chuckling, and grandly gesturing with his smoking hand. He did this right after the announcer barked that no smoking would occur in the O2 venue on Tuesday, August 21, 2007. The audience laughed with him, and the next day's newspaper headlines blared out his (and Ronnie's) disregard for the rules. At a later show, rather than lighting the cig, he put it whole into his mouth as if to eat it.

Many fans do like everyone in the band, pointing to the synergy of The Glimmer Twins and the crucial contributions of Charlie's drumming and Ronnie's playing and energy to the band's mix. When asked for her favorite Rolling Stone, Cindy P says, "I am a Stones Chick," rather than a Mick or Keith chick.

Part I: The 60s and 70s, through the early 80s

Sexuality of Stones Onstage and Audience Reactions

While sex and drugs have been part of the Stones legacy, evident in their song lyrics, their sexual exploits and occasional drug busts, they have also turned up in stories of fans going to concerts. Among the band members, front man Mick Jagger manifests the sexual aspects most boldly and consciously, with Keith as his foil performing nearby. The feelings the fans gain from the performers mix with their own to bounce back and affect the performers, returning the energy radiating from the stage, in a feedback loop between audience and musicians.

Mick has practiced the art of seduction, comparing himself to a female stripper in his engagement with the audience. He created a style in which he enters a show fully dressed, shedding some of his clothes as the show moves along. His costumes mirror the evolution of his persona, including his more androgynous years. His Uncle Sam outfit of 1969, for example, had two-tone pants studded up the sides, a wide, jeweled belt, a scoop-necked top, and a long scarf. The red, white and blue flag hat topped his hair, grown longer with the times. The terms "Mick Jagger" and "androgynous" became almost synonymous, his name used to explain the idea. A few years later, he and the rest of the band prefigured the glam rockers use of make-up and more feminine garments with gauzier materials in lighter shades. Keith and Ronnie have written how they often borrowed their girlfriends' clothes.

In the later years, Mick returned to his younger days wearing relatively mainstream clothing if in brighter colors and skintight fit. The prototype outfit for some years is a jacket over a long-sleeved shirt or t-shirt with slim pants and his black Nikes. A nod to his previous stripping down is how he removes his jacket, sometimes undoing the shirt buttons, but not taking the shirt off as in the shows of the earlier tours, before the 1990s. For a while he would pull up the t-shirt to flash his nipples, as if inviting females in the audience to imitate him. He sometimes still pulls the jacket off one shoulder or both of them. To most of his audience, from what I can tell, his performance comes across as predominantly masculine, with his hard-edged facial expressions, his singing, and song lyrics, though flirtatious elements appear. He is known to swivel his hips and shake his ass, walking on tiptoe at times. To me, whichever private experimentations away from heterosexuality did or did not occur in the early days are overshadowed by public gestures for the pure entertainment value. For example, Mick licked a surprised Ronnie on the lips on a 1978 *Saturday Night Live* show. While he has suggestively danced with Billy Preston in the 70s, in more recent days he seems to prefer physical contact with Lisa Fischer during "Gimme Shelter" or holding special guest Christina Aguilera tightly, standing behind her, singing "Live With Me" in 2006.

One woman online calls Mick "OrgasMICK" and other females have said there is no point in trying to have actual sex with anyone after a show because you are so spent from being there. Here are some characterizations of Mick's sexual appeal:

Mick soon became my favorite, partly for his teasing and taunting sexual and defiant manner.

Mick - first because he's hotter, I'm more of a front-man kinda girl anyway and secondly I like his personality more.....sexier voice as well.

Mick was my favorite for many, many years. What woman doesn't find him attractive and sexy. Look at his moves, and when he plays the harp, awesome. I felt he was the heart and soul of the Stones.

You Get What You Need

Mick...I still find him to be incredibly sexy. Only he can mesmerize me... the others can't.

Man, I have been a Mick girl since age 14. Nobody did better justice to a jumpsuit, and nobody wore eye-makeup better. Nobody commanded a stage better - and looked as good doing it! Mick has always been the stuff of dreams - and fantasies :evil

These statements wouldn't surprise Mick, and yet, he would likely appreciate this kind of feedback. On the other hand, some women find Keith even sexier:

Keith has always seemed the most approachable - and genuine. His earthiness is just as sexy as mick's "bourgeois-ness".

I mean he is so, I guess fluid when he plays and honestly in the seventies I don't think there were many attractive junkies and yet Keith was still the absolute sexiest!!! Amazing.

*From the late 60s on throughout the entire 70s Keith was the f****** hottest and sexiest man walking this planet!!*

Keith has said in *Life* that he couldn't "get laid" at all before the Stones, and then "we were it" and he couldn't keep the girls away. He would tell them he was leaving in the morning, on tour, and they would say, "but I *like* you."

Turning to snapshots of what fans have seen in the moment during early tours, ugotthesilver talks about his first show in 1975 when he and his friend decided to move from their seats at back of the lower level for a close-up view the band.

We were able to get right in front of the stage. I was looking at Mick, looking up at him. I saw how into being on stage he really was. I saw the phallus. I was looking at Keith.

I spent about a third of that concert right up front with the stage pressing into my chest. You could still do that in those days. Right in front of Keith. I can tell you, because I saw it with my own eyes that Mick was clearly getting off sexually on the audience in that era. I'm sure that's at least a part of what made him such an amazing frontman.

Remembering that this was the tour with the giant blow-up phallus during "Star Star," ugotthesilver said that this second night in Philly was "an extraordinary experience," for a long time one of his ten greatest shows.

When Fred H heard the same song "Star Star" or Starfucker" at an indoor show in New Orleans among the 83,173 people counted, he thought, "Jesus Christ, it takes balls to do this in front of all these people." Ahmet Ertegun had insisted on the change in title from the original "Starfucker" even though the lyrics repeat the word in the chorus many times, its verses describing various sex acts. It was 1978 and Fred was hooked.

In the early 70s, Daniel Teafoe recalls his second show in Woodfield, Illinois. He remarked that his childhood was gone at 14, after his first show in 1969. In Woodfield, when the Stones came out, they had glitter coming out of their hair as they shook it to a packed crowd of people: "The whole place went nuts." Daniel spoke of their costumes, the way they looked, and the heat.

It was over 100 degrees...Mick's costume started to tear... We were soaking wet in two songs... You were in extreme body contact. You couldn't be any closer without it being obscene...you were in overload...it couldn't have been any more base.

At the end of "Midnight Rambler," people were passing out from dehydration when Mick took a clear jug with a handle to the front of the stage, and sprinkled cold water on the front row of the audience. Daniel was splashed with the water, and loved it.

On the same tour, Rockman in Melbourne Australia talked about the 100 degree heat also. He said the show on February 13, 1973 had a "special edge" with the stage lighting. Mick looked like "PURE SLUT," wrote Rockman, next to Keith who "really did look pure evil."

Drug Use by Band and Fans

The drug busts of The Rolling Stones enhanced their outlaw image, and fortunately, Mick and Keith's first sentences in London were overturned after each spent a night in jail. Their further encounters with the law on drug charges, one more by Mick, and four more by Keith were either turned into fines, dismissed, reduced, or became stints in rehab so neither ever did more prison time. With the help of a psychiatrist, Brian Jones escaped a long sentence for his second offense, but couldn't tour with the band overseas. Ronnie was detained in Fordyce, Arkansas with Keith for several hours after police impounded their rented Impala, before they were both let go.

The drugs taken by fans prior to or at shows and the rumored drugs ingested by the performers go hand-in hand, especially during the earlier years of the band. All the band members ingested psychedelic drugs, along with alcohol and most likely amphetamines and cocaine. The main issue in Stones history outside of Brian's near-constant drug-taking was Keith's intake of heroin throughout the 70s. In the present, Ronnie's sobriety after prior problems with cocaine and long-term alcoholism seems lasting after his latest stint in rehab. That and Keith's near-death head injury put an end to excessive use of intoxicants pre-show and possibly post-show for both. Keith has stated in the manner of Mark Twain that reports of his abstinence have been greatly exaggerated, reputedly having given up cocaine, but not alcohol or marijuana. Charlie apparently quit all drugs, after a struggle with a heroin addiction for a few years in the 1980s. Mick partakes in light social drinking, and neither Mick nor Charlie smokes tobacco, unlike Ronnie and Keith.

Returning to events of the early days, the story of Altamont is still told, probably gathering more words than any other rock show in Western culture, with the exception of Woodstock. The two mass festivals have become for some, iconic representations of the best and worst of the countercultural epoch, "the 60s." The two events occurred the same year, within a little over three months of each other in 1969, Woodstock in mid-August, in New York, and Altamont in early December in California. The Rolling Stones were at Altamont, not Woodstock, playing when a Hell's Angel killed Meredith Hunter with a knife, documented by the Maysles brothers' documentary *Gimme Shelter* (1970). One element of the free festival at this racetrack twenty miles north of San Francisco was the prevalence of drugs.

Living in the Bay area, diane d, in all small letters, as she is known online, spoke of the "huge music explosion in San Francisco" in the mid to late 1960s when "everybody was going to dances, and everybody was listening to the music." Remarking that the Stones hadn't toured for about three years, she went to her first show in November 9, 1969 in Oakland, California. This tiny young woman, with her very long brown hair in bangs, a style she still wears today, found herself less than a month later at Altamont Speedway at the infamous, free, festival-type concert added after the official tour ended. Friends with Rock Scully who managed the Grateful Dead, the band that suggested the Hell's Angels for security, diane was part of the backstage crew. She said:

We'd spent the night, from five in the afternoon the day before, very stoned, up all night. There were all kinds of drugs. Then the music started, after we had a few minutes of sleep. We saw all these people coming over the hill and thought, oh, no, that's it. There was a bad vibe from the beginning. I was able to go

backstage and sort of hideout, and when the Stones came on,
somebody grabbed my hand and pulled me up on the stage.

She described the Hell's Angels "running amok...kicking people." She
went back and forth between the stage and the safer place in the
equipment truck. Her boyfriend eventually found her, suggested they go,
and they left the concert. Part of the problem for her was

...we were so close, right there where all the bad things were
going on... The Stones played fantastic, wonderfully, when they
managed to play. It was very stop and start in the beginning.
They were really playing very, very, very well...Mick Taylor had
just joined the band...

Mixed into the countercultural "scene of sex, drugs, and rock 'n roll" in
San Francisco, the Angels

were outlaws. They had never really caused any trouble before...
something was going on.

Part of it was the guys who were the real leaders weren't there.
It was just these lower-echelon guys and they were all so crazed
on drugs.

With the Angels' inexperienced members in charge and potential
recruits there to watch over their motorcycles, all carrying weighted
pool cues, and the rumored "bad acid," alcohol and speed permeating
the crowd's sensibilities, the presumed mellowness of the hippie culture
never sets in. Quite the contrary, according to one writer (Spitz, 2011):
"As the day progresses, with drug-taking and drinking by the Angels
and members of the audience, the mood turns ugly" (p 151). Mick was
punched as he made his way to the stage, and an Angel fought with
Marty Balin of the Jefferson Airplane and knocked him out while Balin
was trying to help someone else. Notoriously, the Grateful Dead left the
area by helicopter before they were due to perform. The desolate, rocky

locale of Altamont was chosen only 24 hours before the show, replacing the original destination of Golden Gate Park and then Sears Point Raceway where a crew had begun to build the stage. While the presence of the Hell's Angels monitoring the crowd was probably the major cause of the negative happenings, the drugs distributed and consumed were a part of the whole scene. Nonetheless, people not near the stage area purportedly had a good time at the festival.

In the early 70s, bringing up how the band's run-ins with law enforcement affected the audience, FarEastBam (Shigeo) from Shidoobee noted that the Stones were supposed to come to Japan for the first time in 1973 for a concert in Nippon Budokan Hall. The show sold out but FarEastBams's older sister managed to get one ticket. However, the show was canceled, Shigeo said, because of "Mick's drug problem." The Japanese Foreign Ministry cited Mick's prior drug charges in the UK to bar his entrance.

Fans speaking of drugs in the era recall their own experiences hearing the band at home, or with friends. Gerardo of Rocks Off learned to like the band from listening to records played by his older brother, first singles and then the first album he heard, *Aftermath*. After the brother ran away leaving his albums, and then returning to pick them up, Gerardo had to buy his own, beginning with 1978's *Sticky Fingers*. His English wasn't good enough to understand all the lyrics so he had to use his "imagination" to interpret the "idiomatic expression." He saw the music as a background for getting stoned at parties, the lyrics portraying a "rebel view" of life. TomL remembered eating hash brownies in a buddy's basement to watch *Gimme Shelter* around 1974. Raining Blimps couldn't get tickets to the 1972 show, sold by lottery. That year his next-door neighbor in the dorm at Ohio University was "an insane fan" from New York. They went through copies of the live album *Ya-Yas* "like candy." He and a few other friends in the dorm went to the '75 show in Cleveland together. They called their part of the dorm "the midnight ramblers" area. When they partied in someone else's room, they would "smuggle out a reefer."

Blind Mellon (Marc) and Stones75 (Scotty) had drug-related episodes at concerts on the 1975 tour. Highlighting how both band and audience members had likely taken LSD, Blind Mellon went to a June show in Buffalo, with tickets through a tour company,

> *on a party bus, with an all-inclusive price, with the bus ride, and beer...*

> *This show was not on the original schedule and was the last North American show before they headed to South America. That show was outdoors and it's rumored that the band dropped LSD before the show.*

As it turned out, the band had abandoned their dates in Mexico, Brazil and Argentina, substituting four U.S. concerts, citing concerns of security and changing currencies. The second Buffalo show in August, their last date of the tour, became widely known as the "acid show" by fans who attended. Some said Mick, Keith and Ronnie took LSD, and reportedly many fans in the 95,000-person crowd joined them. Keith's arrest for possession of LSD and other drugs a year later supported the rumors. Audience members who had taken "bad acid" on "bad trips" were seen carried out of the crowd on stretchers. The giant phallus and the mobile lotus platform from which Mick emerged highlighted the visual spectacle of the '75 tour.

Stones75 pointed out that the 1975 tour was the band's first outing with Ronnie Wood. He was 15, curious about how the band would play with Ronnie, after Mick Taylor's departure. Charlie Daniels and J. Geils preceded The Stones onstage, as 50 to 60, 000 people boogied in the hot sun. Stones75 and friends found themselves in the company of a stranger who stayed with them all day. Just as they were getting fed up with this guy mooching off their stashes of pot and hash, the "mooch" produced

the biggest pile of coke I had ever seen, nudging me to indulge, and what the hell, it was the 4th and a Stones party so we got fueled...The Stones came on blaring, no, make that snarling.

In Memphis, he and his friends had ticketed seats at the back of Memorial Stadium, now very high on cocaine, as well as the marijuana and hashish. Not happy with their view from where they were, stones75 talked one of his friends into testing out the lighting tower perimeter, and he started climbing the fence, before he was quickly chased down.

Others saw it and tried and that was our chance...We were coked up and ready and scrambled the fence at the first distraction. Soon scores overwhelmed security and were right behind us and it was a scramble to the top. I'm climbing as fast as I can.

He heard a voice calling him close by who turned out to be a friend from Louisville he didn't know was there, with another guy he knew, both climbing the fence with him. He had a real purpose now, "two songs into The Stones, and anarchy reigns." They made it to the top, right under the lighting platform.

There are tons of people under us, mass confusion, but we are sitting high and tight with a birdseye view of the festivities. It was great !!! The guys manning the lights are hanging over the edge looking down on us pleading with us to get down cuz the tower was now swaying noticeably...

They had nowhere to go from their perch, and could see the second tower being swarmed by more fans. They realized what they were doing "wasn't exactly safe."

Anyway after a couple of songs Mick looks at us and implores us to get down saying "If we knew you were gonna climb it we would have made it safer" or some such bullshit , it's on the boot which I can provide.

Stones75 described how it took the overweight security guards a long while to climb up below them and start smacking their shoes with billy bats, demanding them to "dethrone." They stayed for four or five songs "and we weren't arrested." He took his online name from going to that show.

Arthur has tales from Philly in '78 and '81 at the Capitol Center in Langley, Maryland, right after the pay-per-view in Hampton, Virginia. A Philly show in the rain was Arthur's first live experience in 1978. The atmosphere then was "more 60s, 70s, a lot of drugs" used openly, "a lot of drinking."

Everyone was very friendly. The whole football field was tents and sleeping bags. The whole place was general admission. The concert started at noon. Foreigner was there. The Stones came out at six o'clock. I thought it was the best concert I'd ever seen in my life, in a football field at the fifty-yard line. The sound was awesome.

Back then he noted that they played at a faster speed, Keith going so fast that "Mick would have to work to keep up with him".

Arthur backtracked to explain how he happened to be at that show. He said "about ten of us went up there from Washington D. C., borrowing a van from a Catholic priest." With a full cooler and "all the kinds of marijuana you could have," they left at four in the morning, drinking and smoking pot. They were "ready to rock out." When they got there

Andrea Baker

Everybody was bonding, asking "Where'ya from?" It was a big group affair. You could walk around with the feeling of what's happening. People would give you a toke.

They watched the all-day concert, and then The Stones played sixteen songs, most of them from the new album. Arthur thought it might be their last tour.

Going to three concerts in a row in Langley, Maryland, Arthur discovered that once they see you coming back, "they really recognize you...they want to see the regulars." He started dressing a certain way after that, wrapped up in The Rolling Stones. Arthur felt that on the '81 tour "Keith wanted to do the indoor thing, and Mick wanted to make money," so they played both indoor shows and stadiums.

By '81, smoking marijuana was not so accepted in a concert hall as before. The shows were turning into family events. On the floor people could "do anything," but Arthur and his friends were on the side, passing a joint back and forth.

Mick walks up to Keith and says into the microphone, "They're smoking pot". Keith walks up and gives you that wink, that look. I've never sat more than eight rows away. Without that, it's not worth it.

He described perfectly why many fans feel they have to be so close to the stage to really enjoy the show, once they experience the personal interaction between the band and audience members.

For a 1982 show in Gothenburg, Sweden, Vilhelm observed how before there was the internet, everything was "much more exciting," as people waited for a band to come around," with a "bit of mystery" about what was to come. For the second show there, Vilhelm was the first one at the stadium at 9 a.m., waiting all day. At the show, still his favorite, he felt the playing was "very sloppy. Keith was dead drunk."

112

Also in Europe in 1982, Aiden saw the band at Slane Castle in Ireland. He thought all of the opening bands were "pretty terrible" and The Rolling Stones "didn't sound that great either, " although he "still liked them." He noticed the large number of "wasted people in Ireland at those kinds of shows" like Slane and the Knebworth Festival, also outdoors. He and his contingent only had one beer a piece.

Issues with Parents, Schools, and Spouses

When very young, some fans cut school to go see the Stones. MRDEEEE (Bob) was just thirteen when he decided he had to see the band in 1965 at the three-day Palm Beach Pop Festival, on the bill with Jimi Hendrix and Janis Joplin. He saw them with Brian Jones and then later on, twice with Mick Taylor. Trouble brewed when the Stones were delayed:

> *The Stones were supposed to close the festival on Sunday night. Their plane broke down and they were eight hours late...Most people left-- there were less than a few thousand left. We were cold and wet, miserable...*

When their parents wouldn't give them permission to go to the festival, MRDEEEEE and his friend pulled the time-honored teenage trick of each saying he was staying at the friend's house. That might have worked out, if the Stones weren't leaving so late from Boston, not coming on until 4:30 a.m. By the time the boys got home on Monday afternoon

> *the school had called, "Where's your son?" The police had been called. Everybody pretty much figured out where we were...That was the last time I got my ass kicked*

or any whipping from his parents, said MRDEEEEE. By his 70s shows he was old enough to go without either his parents' help or their wrath.

Seeing them on *The Ed Sullivan Show*, founder of Shidoobee Stonesdoug has loved them since he heard "Time is on Our Side". The music "wasn't a conservative type music...it was a little wild, maybe," he remembers. Their dress was scruffy. They performed in sweatshirts, instead of suits like other bands of the era.

> *Everyone knew I was the Stones guy in high school. I had some buttons I would wear. My father didn't like the band at all. My mother liked some of the music..."As Tears Go By"...*

Growing up in Cherry Hill, New Jersey, he had just completed his first year in prep school in Philadelphia in 1966 at age fifteen when he heard they were playing close by in the Marine Ballroom at the Steel Pier in Atlantic City. In spite of his father's distaste for the band, he accepted a free pass from a friend who owned the Pier. Doug went to his first show: "I got up to the front. I was mesmerized."

Criss Cross Mind of Chicago either "nicked or bought" all the American LPs on their release after he saw the band on the Ed Sullivan show. His parents would not support him attending the Airie Crown Theater show on Lake Shore Drive in 1966. He had to wait until 1969 to see his first show. Elmo Lewis from IORR happily received the *Goat's Head Soup* album for his fourteenth birthday, his parents unaware of the "starfucker" lyrics of "Star Star." Mi jim's father found The Rolling Stones "menacing" when he saw them on the TV show *Hullabaloo*. He didn't "think they would last." His parents weren't about to let him go in a car to see the band when he was 14, but he did make the Detroit, Michigan show in 1975.

Playing Keith in the tribute band, The Glimmer Twins, Bernie was only ten when the Tattoo You tour started in 1981. One of his older brothers was able to see the show. When they opened the tour in Philadelphia, this announcement came over the loudspeaker: "Anyone who isn't in school tomorrow better have a doctor's excuse because we know there's a Stones show" going on. Then in '89 when had just started his performance career, "cutting my teeth on the cover circuit," he was there in Philly for opening night.

On spousal disinterest or opposition, I married a guy many times more likely to go to the symphony or Judy Collins than a rock concert in Cleveland, Ohio where we moved for his work. I remember clearly that he loved the photo in *Goat's Head Soup* so much that he put it up on the wall of his den. I wasn't that crazy about seeing the close-up of the animal's head in the boiling pot, eyes half open, but I figured, well, at least he likes something about the Stones. I grew to accept the portrait of the pinned-up goat, almost fondly. I didn't get to any shows until much later on, well after we split up.

EG Tom's ex-wife thought he was just plain "nuts" over The Stones because of how he "always played them, all the time." Thru and Thru's husband Walt didn't share his wife's love for the band, asking why would they want to go, and thinking, anyway, they were too old to be fans. When he saw them on a pay-for-view show, he was surprised at how good they were.

Part II: They're Back, 1989 Through the 90s

When the band finished its last show in Europe at Roundhay Park in Leeds, West Yorkshire, England on July 25th, 1982 for over 120,000 fans, no one suspected they'd have to wait until the end of the decade for another show. Performances after that, but before 1989 contained one or more members, but not the entity called The Rolling Stones, with all of the four core players. "Mick and Keith had been feuding," says Shidoobee mi jim. Fenway Joe liked their early 80s album *Dirty Work*, but heard the band members were not getting along: "This was it. It's all over," he assumed.

Finally, after a reported thaw between Mick and Keith through phone calls finessed by peacemaker Ronnie Wood, the band regrouped to go on the road again in 1989. Fans breathed a collective sigh of relief, not knowing what to expect, just happy that the band appeared intact. To date, this break remains the longest period in the band's history when they haven't played publicly, followed by another lengthy period between summer 2005 and late fall 2012, after the publication of Keith's *Life* in 2010.

For MRDEEEEE, the wait until 1989 was long enough that he chose to travel to eleven different shows, all the way to the west coast, down to Texas, and back to New Orleans from his home base in Florida.

I thought it might be the last time. The Stones were fighting. Jagger and Richards were making solo albums, and taking pot shots at each other. Jagger wanted to tour by himself. He went to Japan in '88. When he tried to book a tour here in the States, none of the promoters were interested.

In '89 rumors started to circulate, said Fenway Joe, that Mick and Keith were going to do something, in spite of some of the quotes that he had heard such as Keith saying that if he ever sees Mick Jagger on the street, he's "going to kick his butt" in Joe's words. He ended up going to Boston, attending three stadium shows. He did "a lot of work" to get tickets, including those to a show taped for pay-per-view in Miami, and also to shows in Tampa and Gainesville.

Yesterday's Papers had waited for a comeback, which finally happened, seven years after their last show in Europe. It was "like coming back from the dead" when they reappeared for a tour. He couldn't get tickets when they went on sale, and wouldn't pay the scalpers for the Foxboro shows, so he "pretty much listened to the show outside." Mi jim also had difficulty finding tickets because "the buzz" for the 1989 shows in Detroit "was incredible." He and his brother went to the second night at the stadium with "nosebleed" tickets. "We could touch the roof of the Silverdome."

Recurring themes in this period following the band members' reconciliation after their rift were problems between security and fans, tensions among fans, or between fans and the band, and, more positively, fans beginning to meet other fans through publications and the start of the internet. By this time, the band began to name each album and its accompanying tour with specific titles and visual motifs related to the design of the stage and the images on fan gear rather than just for the geographical locations they played. They came up with the *Steel Wheels/Urban Jungle* tour (1989-1990), *Voodoo Lounge* (1994-95), *Bridges to Babylon* (1997-1999), and *No Security* (1999), between the first and second legs of *BtB*.

Conflicts of Audience with Security and Others

Like many others, Little Queenie (LQ) thought she'd have a chance to see the band soon after the '81 tour. She asked for *Hot Rocks* for Christmas that year, at 15, and would buy mostly bootlegs and used vinyl. She remembers when they broke up in the mid-80s, finding herself getting immersed in "60s leftover stuff". The city where she lives, Chicago, "is really a classic area" for music. For the 1989 tour, she knew she had to go, at first getting scalped tickets from the newspaper for 200 dollars. She ended up selling them, buying tickets elsewhere at a reasonable price.

Once at the show, she doesn't recall if she was screaming and yelling or not, in her "kind of a crappy seat." She blew Mick a kiss as he came down the runway and he blew her a kiss back. She was in the front row of the balcony at the stadium when she jumped to her feet to dance. The guy behind her asked her to sit down. She told him "no," because "It's not a movie," prompting him to seek out security. During "Tumbling Dice" LQ argued over whether she should sit down or not, "fighting with a security guard" who said she should. She refused and stayed standing, but she said the episode ruined the song.

117

At her second show at the Compaq Center in Houston in 1998, Blue Lena and her friends collided with a female fan who did not want to stand while watching the concert or have anyone in front of her standing. As soon as Keith stepped onstage the "fat old bitch" who "thought she was at a Wayne Newton show" called security on them. When they didn't comply with the direction to sit down, "the security lady called the cops on us!" They were promptly escorted out of the venue. Ironically that day's edition of *The Houston Chronicle* had featured them in an article about RS fans. At the time, BL wrote on her website that

> *the Stones awesome performance was marred by overzealous security guards & the lame Houston crowd. My friends & I were thrown out for three songs Friday night for STANDING UP during the show!!! Can you believe it? I still can't & I plan to get retribution & make the Stones aware of how poorly their biggest fans were treated at the Compaq Center. Some of us had travelled many miles to see these shows...*

Another audience problem happened for BL when she managed to get a wristband for the Shepherd's Bush show in the UK in June1999, but this time the experience was worth the tension. She and two friends arrived at the line at Tower Records in London at 4:30 a.m., with a stop in Cambridge following the Sheffield show. Waiting for tickets and wristbands for over six hours, she and two friends received numbers 111, 112, and 113. When she finally she got in, after another long wait from 5 a.m. the next day, she went immediately over to buy a t-shirt. For the show, she found a spot located five people away from the stage in front of Keith. The two problems were she couldn't see the stage for most of the show, and when the Stones came out, the crowd pushed and shoved toward the front, crushing bodies together, and even lifting people off their feet. The pressure from the crowd led a fan near BL to fall down in a faint, with the crowd passing his body over their heads to a security person on the other side.

You Get What You Need

On the plus side, along with just getting into the 2000-person venue, talking to fans she knew and others in line, BL notes the thrill of hearing rarities played during the set, such as "Melody," played during the *No Security* tour, "I Got the Blues," "Moon is Up," and, from the *Voodoo Lounge* album, "Brand New Car". As the "culmination of that experience" in the UK, after three other shows there, Shepherd's Bush represented something she "never thought she would attain," entrance to a club gig.

NeverBreak had a chance to witness hassle from border guards, and later, some unrest within the audience when fans became cranky while waiting for the band to come on, before their anger turned to ecstasy. This was at her first show, in Czechoslovakia, though she had been a fan since the start. NeverBreak didn't really have the cash and wasn't around towns where concerts were happening. Then in 1990, when she was much older and had relocated outside of the States, the band held a concert in Prague. Communism had collapsed, and "these countries were still in the process of forming their identity." One day a friend of hers in show business had organized a bus to take people to the Prague show, and NeverBreak said, "Hell, yeah!" to the six-hour trip. The arrangement was that the ticket would serve as a visa too, "such an incredible thing for people who had been so restricted." This was the "mind set," says NeverBreak:

> *Rock and roll had freed us, baby, and who's going to show us how it's done...To see these people, that a ticket should get them across the border...The border guards gave us a hard time, which heightens the joy of it, when they have to let the bus through.*

The Strahov Stadium could hold 300,000 but let in only 130,000 people, with "ten toilets," describes NeverBreak. People were packed in and then Václav Havel showed up, the President who had displaced the Communist regime only eight months earlier. The entire stadium stood up and said his name in unison, "Václav." "It was incredible to see the love they have for that man." The fans became irritated with the long wait for the Stones after the warm up acts, and then it started raining. "Everybody was furious," and then they finally came out, playing "Start Me Up," continuing for two and a half hours.

From the first note, NeverBreak was crying. She described a moment when the rain stopped right when Mick began singing at the top of the tower where he can't be seen. Keith was singing too and at the end of the song, his arms were curled around the mic. "There was such an outpouring from the crowd...of love." Then Keith did "Happy," fitting the mood. Fans from Russia and Czechoslovakia had little contact with Western music, only accidentally, if they knew someone with access to it, said NeverBreak. When the band performed "You Can't Always Get What You Want" for this crowd of people in Prague who had "spent all their lives waiting for a chance to see any big name band," the reaction was tumultuous. Singing in unison, these fans felt they had finally gotten what they needed. Keith talked from the stage about how people there had broken down walls, broken down barriers. NeverBreak quoted Giorgio Gomelsky who said back in the early 60s that the band's energy has given everybody "courage for years and years and years." NeverBreak said that we should know that The Stones' mission is to "touch as many people as possible."

As a side note, the British dramatist Tom Stoppard later wrote a play I saw in New York, *Rock 'n' Roll* (2006), about political and cultural change in Eastern Europe during the time period from 1968 through 1990. The play used Stones music during the scene changes, along with songs by the Czech band The Plastic People of the Universe, who gave a live performance at the premiere in Prague. Set in two places, the dialogue shifted back and forth between characters in Prague, Czechoslovakia where Stoppard was born to those in Cambridge, England. A gentleman on a fan board who had seen the show before me noticed errors in the production, including the playing of "You Got Me

Rocking'" at the ending of Stoppard's play in 1990, four years before the song was first released. That was an intentional error, as we suspected, and Stoppard clarified in an email. He chose the song recorded live in Amsterdam with accompanying crowd noise on *No Security* (1998) to represent the tone of that point in the play, the climax, a mass celebration of freedom at the Prague concert attended by NeverBreak. Mick Jagger saw it but he was kind enough not to mention it, Stoppard wrote me. Another minor point caught by the discerning fan was the inaccuracy of the credits for who was playing on the original version of "It's Only Rock 'n Roll" listed on a slide shown during the show. After seeing a photo of it, Stoppard responded that he would ask the sound designer who did the projections to change it.

Meeting Other Fans: Pre-internet to the Beginnings of Online Communication

A relatively small number of people were online before the first internet browser Mosaic changed the internet in 1994. Academics and techies had formed newsgroups based on common interests, real-time chat lines (IRCs or internet relay chats) and local bulletin board systems (BBSs). In the 80s and into the 90s, Bill German mailed out his newsletter *Beggar's Banquet* to subscribers, as did Bjornulf Vic who sent the paper version of *It's Only Rock 'n Roll* to fans on his list.

In the late 20th and very early years of the 21st, the fans interviewed here could join online groups including Bjornulf's online IORR, Rocksoff (RO) begun by Jaxx, Voodoochile and Gazza, Doug Potash's Shidoobee and Steve Portigal's private email list, Undercover (UC). The "unholy trinity" of RO met on the *Bridges to Babylon* thread of the original message board at the online Rolling Stones site that its managers deleted some years ago. They thought this official site "wasn't doing enough to keep fans up to date with the tour so we set up our own message board" originally called "Goin' Home" with Linda instigating the move that spring. She quit because of too much spamming, so the three founded RO. Stonesdoug was on AOL on a thread for fans of The Rolling Stones when he disagreed with one of the members. He decided to spin off from there to start his own board "Shidoobee," joined by some of the AOL people.

What began to happen was that fans could meet each other online and offline, and communicate their passion for the Stones outside of the older, formalized fan clubs headquartered in one city or another. The process greatly accelerated after the turn of the century as fan groups established an identity online, easily found through search engines, and more of the populace became aware of their presence. The online meeting places affected how fans became aware of tickets and gathered before and after shows (see Chapter Four). Here fans explain how they encountered each other during the 90s.

By the time *Steel Wheels* came around, Steve Portigal and his friends all liked the music and were old enough to go. Before that, none of them had seen the band because they were too young to travel to Buffalo in 1981, the nearest place the Stones played. They went to the opening shows in Philly in 1989, and three of the four nights in Toronto, where he was living at the time. That marked him as "a weirdo to everybody else," but gave the bespectacled Steve a solid background to head a private group and then an email list he started for fans in the early 90s called Undercover (UC). Between 1989 and 1994, he moved out to the west coast, seeing the band in Oakland where they did four dates. He became more of a "hungry fan", seeking out more songs he wanted to hear.

In the Bay area, Steve met other fans, and they would distribute extra tickets to each other and drive to shows together. They would get each other onto the floor by using ticket stubs and taking empty seats. In '97, he started buying plane tickets, attending the opener in Chicago, and joining the big fan parties there. One fan had people come to his house, and another local organized a party in a bar. Because of online communication, there was, in Steve's words,

> *a collective critical mass of fandom, people who all knew each other but had never met...people from Europe...one or two had met.. It was insane. It was really fun...We are still running jokes from that week.*

He didn't see those people again until they made it out to the west coast for shows.

During *Voodoo Lounge*, Chicago_Dave had moved back to Chicago from the west coast. Now there was the internet starting up for greater access to information, and cable television with the music channels. For the '97 tour, Dave found the private email list Undercover where fans planned parties, and he went on the IORR board too. His finances "weren't the greatest", and then he found out that the band was coming to Chicago to open, even doing a surprise show at a small club. He didn't make it inside of the "Double Door" concert, but he left work a little early to find himself standing across the street from the place when they opened the doors. He heard the whole show from outside, and saw a couple of band members getting out of their cars. He ended up hanging around at rehearsals at Soldier Field stadium for three days with a dozen or so other people from around the world.

Michael from Germany recalls his first concert in Frankfort in May 1990 on the *Urban Jungle* tour. He found it "fantastic to see them live," since he was a big fan as a pre-teen in the early 1970s. He joined Undercover in '93, which was why he got tickets for Chicago in the States, because of a posting by a tour operator there. From the time he became a member, he often gathered with people from the UC list. They would meet at the gate, going in together, and he would sleep at the place of a person on the list. In '94 in Chicago, attending the show with an old buddy, he met a few people from Undercover who also met in

123

London for shows the next summer. For the European leg of the tour in '95, he went to Cologne, Berlin, and Manheim, as well as London. In 2010, I met Michael, extremely warm and friendly, yet soft-spoken, who had traveled from Germany with his girlfriend to a gathering in Clarksdale, Mississippi arranged by UC members to explore the historical roots of American blues in the southern U.S.

Attending her first European shows, two in London, and Sheffield and Edinburgh, Nandita, a dark-haired fan only 5'1" tall from Puerto Rico met a lot of Undercover people. She met some Americans in London who became "pretty good friends." It was the first time she experienced seeing the Stones with an online community. Two people, a couple, had organized parties after the shows, and had chartered "a big, red bus...which was great, to take us to the shows at Wembley," says Nandita. In '99, she really wanted to go to *No Security*. She attended her first official UC gathering in Chicago.

Fenway Joe and Carl first met offline and grew closer over the years. Joe had met Carl the Lobsterman and his ex-wife in 1997 at a minor league baseball game when Carl saw a Stones patch on Joe's baseball hat. When a Stones show was canceled and then rescheduled in Montreal in 1998, Joe called Carl from Quincy, Massachusetts. He and his then-wife met the bus and they all took the bus trip to Montreal. Exile Brian from Shidoobee was on the bus too with his boom box. They made bets on what time the bus would stop in front of their hotel and Fenway Joe won. Carl said

That was probably one of the best shows. I always claimed that "Miss You" that night roared....Bobby started playing the sax. It was good from the get-go. The next morning in Montreal...there was this guy with a cord jacket on. His license plates say "Shattered" and "Shidoobee." This was the first time that one of us has seen Doug.

Stonesdoug wears a Levi jacket with two license plates attached to the back, to broadcast his allegiance to the band. He started in 1978 with the Shidoobee plate, adding the Shattered plate in 1989. Asked about the history of the name Shidoobee, Doug says that after hearing the word "shidoobee" in "Shattered" the song, "a bunch of college friends called ourselves shidoobees since the early 1980s and we all had t shirts."

With Joe's wife, they all ended up flying to Wembley Stadium for the European leg of the *Bridges* tour in June 1999. It was Carl's first time overseas. Joe had become his companion for the shows. The couples and a friend of Carl's were tourists in London during the day, recalling that the English liked to play and sing Tom Jones songs. Carl went to check out Wembley, "to see where it was at," taking the underground. At the concert, Carl and Joe spotted Doug for the second time, "the guy with the license plates...sewn on the back of his jacket." Carl also sighted the Vikings crew of fans who back then sported white shirts with "Rolling Stones" spelled out on them. Among other fans he has met, Carl wishes to give a shout-out to the member of Rocks Off, Mark from California, who designed "the unique lobster logo" for Carl's avatar.

Mentioning "all the tech" and the *Steel Wheels* stage, Arthur thought that the band sounded great and thus, "could never play better" than in 1989. But then when the internet came alive for the '94 tour, everything became easier. Arthur says, "I had some friends and went to 15-20 shows...the internet made it so we could all talk to each other and we could follow the band easier."

The internet at the time had newsgroups and private email. On the newsgroups, people would get nasty, start fights and disrupt threads, with no moderation. That's why Stonesdoug decided to start his website later on to have a place where people can talk all over the world without hassles and "he can kick you off" if someone gets insulting, said Arthur. Arthur pointed out that because he was so "tech conscious," Mick really appreciated the internet. Arthur wanted to participate in the internet voting for *Voodoo Lounge* but didn't have a chance to do it.

At fifteen Johnny O went to shows with his dad and his sister in Phoenix in 1997, recalling that how "they exploded" onstage with 'Satisfaction'" was "the coolest thing" he'd ever seen. After another show in 1998 in San Diego where his mom joined the rest of the family, Johnny found the chat room on AOL for The Rolling Stones, meeting Stonesdoug online. When Doug started Shidoobee, Johnny didn't register for a while, not posting as a guest. He met Doug in person in San Jose in 1999. That was when "he really became hooked," gathering with other fans he knew from online. Even though the shows in northern California were cancelled that tour, he sensed "an instant commonality between everyone, and despite only being 17 years old at the time, I felt like I fit in, " said Johnny.

JasontheKeithoholic then only a junior in high school drove in1989 to see the band with Eric Clapton at Shea Stadium. Similar to the meeting of FenwayJoe and Carl, Jason met Stonesdoug not at a show, but at a sporting event. After meeting Stonesdoug at a Giants game in 1997, he started going to shows with him, attending twelve concerts on the *Bridges to Babylon* tour, "all over the east coast," and into Canada.

In 1999, Gerardo from Mexico, Jackie from Colorado, and Gazza from Northern Ireland all traveled to see two shows in Hartford, Connecticut for the first Rocks Off gathering, the first time Gazza had traveled to another country for a show. The idea for RO was born in early '98 when they initially planned to start a message board, not a web site, at the very beginning in July. They changed its name from "Goin' Home" to "Rocks Off" because they liked the title, giving fans a place to go to get their "rocks off" and because the lyrics, "Your mouth don't move but I can hear you speak," are apropos for a message board online, explains Gerardo. Gazza pointed out that their website RO went live online right before the three arrived, two from other countries, to met in person at the Hartford show in the eastern U.S.

Part III: 2002--2007, *Licks* Through *A Bigger Bang*

So many fans had a chance to see the band on the tours in the new century, on *Licks* of 2002 and 2003, and then on *A Bigger Bang*, which wound up running longer than usual due to Keith's accident, from 2005 to 2007. *Licks* had a special feature, an intentional mix of stadiums, arenas and club shows. Rather than the range of individual fans within particular themes, this section of the chapter focuses on fewer fans and their stories of select special events of the two tours: fan participation at small shows, here, a theater show in the Netherlands, and a private show in Germany, adventures at two benefit shows, a gigantic fund-raiser for victims of the SARS disease outdoors in Toronto, and Radio City Music Hall's concert for poor people sponsored by New York City's Robin Hood organization. Fans also participated in two special filming events, in Detroit for the Super Bowl halftime, and in Scorsese's documentary *Shine a Light* at the Beacon Theater, and a preview of previously un-shown footage from 1969 at Madison Square Garden.

The Theater Show: Fred's Adventures in Vredenburg, Netherlands

Fred Hardin had the time of his life at a club show in the Netherlands in 2003 and wrote about it for IORR, Shidoobee and Rocks Off. The following comes from his own piece and from the interview I did with him. He made so many good friends that trip such as Jan from Holland, Stefan from Germany, and Brian from Stones security. To understand Fred is to know what a tremendously nice guy he is, online and offline. He is the first to thank people, the first to commiserate, and in person, this long-haired fellow with touches of gray in his beard is the first to give a hearty hello and a hug. Of all of the shows he has seen, since his first in 1998, his absolute favorite is Vredenburg, a show he almost missed. His icon on Shidoobee is the logo from Amsterdam that year, with cross-stitches in the tongue.

Fred and his wife Teri almost didn't make it to Holland because their flights on Delta's Buddy Pass plan required them to fly stand-by. Checking ahead, they saw plenty of seats, but as the date neared, Amsterdam flights were rapidly filling. Sure enough, when they came to the airport and waited on the long list of hopeful passengers, they were shut out. Rather than giving up, they decided to catch a much less crowded flight to Brussels and go from there. In a nice happening, they were bumped up to business class, allowing them enough comfort to sleep for much of the journey across the pond. They had to make the shows in Amsterdam Arena on August 19 and 20 that they had purchased ten months earlier. In the meantime, the band announced a club show in nearby Utrecht at the Vredenburg Music center that would require standing in line with the chance of attending a very small venue, a fan's dream. Fred had learned much from Bjorulf Vik at IORR about strategies for getting in. The venue would hold 2,000 people, and the presale tickets were gone in 14 minutes.

Unfortunately when arriving in Brussels, planning to take the train to Utrecht, the Hardins found that their luggage had not transferred to their new flight. They filled out the required forms and went by train to the Brussels Central Station, taking a train from there to Rotterdam, transferring to catch yet another train to Utrecht. They made it to Vredenburg at 13:30 or 1:30 pm. Fred had brought other shoes with him, but no extra clothes, while Teri had packed another complete outfit in her carry on. No matter, they were in the line to the club, after departing from their home in Savannah, Georgia at noon the day before, US Eastern time. They joined people from all over the world to sign in on a list, snagging numbers 71 and 72.

Shortly after he knew he was on the list, Fred went and bought a couple of T-shirts so he could have fresh clothes. He then made the fateful acquaintance of a man called Brian, who would play an instrumental role in what happened later that day:

Several times during that first day at Vredenburg I spoke to a real nice guy named Brian who was dressed all in black, I originally thought he must have been part of the lighting crew. I later found out he was part of the Stone's security. Several times that day he had told me that Shirley said there were not going to be any tickets issued at all. He said she is the one who knows.

Fred explained to Brian that "we had just flown from the States to Belgium that morning and then caught 3 trains to Utrecht to try to luck into seeing this incredible event" and they "were not giving up until it was over." Brian smiled, saying nothing. Keeping an appointment to meet up with his friend Rich, Fred walked back to the train station. Rich had been working in the Netherlands for a year, and wanted to go to his first Stones concert. They walked back to the line together and waited all afternoon. No tickets were released to the people in line. Feeling the effects of their travel, and seeing the box office locked at 20:20, Fred and Teri chose to leave the line to go with Rich to his house, about 15 minutes away. They ate at a nearby Turkish restaurant, took showers, washed and dried their clothes and finally got to sleep around midnight.

They had told their new friends from the line they would return around 4:00 a.m., but got there at 6:20 a.m. Fred found out to his surprise that in their absence, the people left in line overnight had started a new list for themselves, ditching the old one. On the new list their numbers dropped from 71 and 72 down to 155, 156 and 157, with Rich. Their chances were not looking as good as yesterday, but Fred understood, since they had vacated their spots. Staying positive, Fred said he was glad to have clean clothes and a place with diehard fans from all over in a great country. Security started grouping people according to their place on the list, beginning with the first 50 numbers. "I must say that there were some pretty happy faces on those people, " said Fred. The

129

day slowly passed, with much talking, smiling, and exchange of email addresses. Fred met fans from Shidoobee he had only known online and from IORR too. He was surprised at the number of fans from the US who had flown in. He also met fans that came from Germany, Norway, Sweden, England, China, Poland, Belgium, and, of course, from the Netherlands, the home country of the show.

Nothing happened for a long while until the security people emerged with the list. To accompanying cheers, they announced that first fifty had tickets for sure. They knew they would be seeing an "incredible once in a lifetime Stones Event!" Security said they would follow the list, with more tickets released, but they didn't have enough for everyone on it. When Fred told Brian what his numbers were, Brian had a "doubtful look on his face, but also a you never know look." The TV news crew was passing through the crowd, doing interviews and taking footage of fans, filming a "lovely lady with beautiful long brown hair" singing "Satisfaction."

A couple of hours went by before a friend of Fred's wife from London came up and said he might have an extra ticket that another friend of his might not need. Fred said that would make "someone out there very happy...Buddy!". They both had a good laugh. He left for a while to return a few hours later, asking if they were interested, telling them what they wanted for it. "Hell, yes!" The friend asked which one of the two they would send in, and Fred told him it would be Teri, his wife. He knew she would give him a detailed description of what he missed, and he had seen three more shows than she had. Like the best husband in the world, he continued,

> *Besides that, it was the only thing I could do. When I told her we had her a Ticket, you should have seen her expression, it was like I had told her she just won a thousand dollars. She was concerned about me not getting in but that was not about to stop her from going in. That's my Baby! I do love her so.*

You Get What You Need

When Teri went to get her band put on with two other women, Fred bought her a Utrecht event t-shirt. "You could not get that smile off that girl's face even if you had tried." She and her new friends went to queue up around 17:00. When he saw Fred, Brian asked him what his number was again, after Fred told him Teri had a ticket. He looked doubtful that tickets would ever be given out with that high a number. Fred assured Brian that he would be "out there waiting" whether he got in or not. His friend Arve MM from Norway had come by often in line, encouraging them to keep up the hope, although he had received his ticket in the first five minutes of the ticket release. At 21:30, Arve had gone in, and the warm-up band was done. Security had reached number 140 on the list, and they said, really meaning it this time, " "That is all the Tickets! We are very sorry but there are no more tickets, I am sorry!" Fred knew he had to rely on Teri for info about the show. Out there when they made this announcement, Brian shook his head as if to say he was sorry, the tickets were all gone. Fred smiled and shrugged his shoulders. "It was a bit crazy around there for a few minutes." Others in line who didn't make the cut were sad, some crying. Some were disbelieving, not wanting to hear that news. Some were even "getting loud" or "downright rude". A few began knocking on the doors as if that would make those inside change their minds.

When they finally locked the doors, Fred was standing near the entrance telling Rich he might want to just go home because Fred would wait for Teri to get out before they headed back to their hotel in Amsterdam. Fred noticed Brian in the street talking to a couple of people, smiled and caught his eye. Brian winked at him and gave a slight tilt of the head as if to say come over here. Just to be sure he hadn't misread Brian, he looked away, and then back, and sure enough, Brian made the same gesture. Fred said, "Holy Shit, Rich, I think we are in!" They walked over to hear where Brian was standing, and when he was done talking to the other people, he turned, walked toward them, and said, "So it's just you two left?" Brian told them, "I think I can get you in." Brian said to wait a few minutes and walk to a certain spot next to a gate. When they arrived there, they saw a couple from San Francisco who they'd met when the couple lined up well after they did. Apparently the couple had talked to Brian too. Brian hand-motioned the four of them inside. They went to the box office, got their tickets, had their wristbands put on, and followed Brian "around a few corners."

....and the next thing you know, WE WERE IN! I could not believe the feeling I had at that time. It was so exciting and so unreal. It was like a dream coming true in the most amazing way I could ever imagine! Getting in to this special show this way was like a wild movie or something. We went in to this beautiful room, I was so amazed at how small it actually was. You could tell by the crowd that at any moment A Hell of a Rock and Roll Event would be taking place.

Fred found Teri, who had seen him and was coming out in the hallway to meet him. When she first saw he had made it in, she had a look on her face this time like "she had won a Million Dollars!

That was one of the best moments of my entire life...We had talked and dreamed of getting into this show for many, many months. We were actually on the other side of the World in a small club show about to see the Greatest Rock and Roll Band in the Whole World. Unbelievable!

Arve was there to witness all this and he and Fred gave each other big hugs. Before Arve, Rich and Fred rushed down to the floor to watch the show. Friends he had made knew his number was high and started giving him hugs and high fives, screaming and shouting, even from the other side of the venue. Friends pulled him up closer to the stage. He ended up "about 1.5 meters from the stage" at the extreme left side, next to a female from Dusseldorf he had seen several times over the last two days. They "danced and jammed the whole show." After the show, amidst the last good-byes to his new friends, Brain came walking by

132

with his headphones and a big smile, looking at Fred as if to say he knows Fred "enjoyed the shit out of that." Fred lunged through the crowd to hug and thank him. Fred's buzz was still going strong outside the venue, when it hit him he had been on his feet nonstop for twelve hours. This "natural high" did not die down for two days, and the vestiges stayed with him for a long time. And he still had two more shows in Amsterdam, in his "Dutch Stones adventure," although one was later cancelled. This was his first club show ever, and in all the tours he had seen in his last quarter century, this was the show of his and Teri's dreams, "the ultimate Stones event."

The Show for German Bankers

The month before *Bigger Bang* ended, a group of German bankers sponsored a private Rolling Stones concert in the Catalan National Art Museum in Barcelona. The Deutsche Bank paid 5.4 million dollars or 2.7 in GBP at the time to allow 500 bank executives in Spain to watch the one-nighter, an 80 minute set. One fan who requests anonymity managed to finally get into the show without a ticket after several hours of trying without success. He dressed appropriately in a white shirt, tie, and "banker's suit," carrying the *Financial Times*.

The SARS Benefit in Toronto and the Show at Radio City Music Hall

A mother of two with short brown hair and fine features, Joyce lived in Ottawa, Canada, when she heard about the July 30, 2003 benefit concert in Toronto. The Stones and other musicians were putting on a festival in Downsview Park to raise funds for the SARS (Severe Acute Respiratory Syndrome) epidemic. The disease had already claimed 27 lives there, hurting the economic health of the city, with tourists afraid to travel to Toronto, even after the World Health Organization had lifted their travel advisory. The band decided to join the line-up of acts charging a very low price of admission. Joyce saw the promo online and bought tickets for herself, and both of her teen-aged kids, not suspecting the adventure that would ensue at her first Stones concert, the biggest ever for Toronto. The show became known as SARSfest or SARSstock because of its size and duration.

After her daughter Cathryn's shift ended at midnight, Joyce picked her up and they parked far away, walking toward the venue past people sleeping there overnight covered by blankets and newspapers. They walked to near the front of the line, entering with two big blankets when the gates opened. The temperature kept going up and up, turning into one of the hottest on record for that day. As the day progressed, People started crowding around their blankets that protected their territory. If you wanted to walk to the concession stand, there was no obvious route. "It was getting harder and harder to get through." People were lined up "like in a refugee camp," she said. She had a case of water, given free to fans, that she put up on her head. She became concerned that her son Jason had headed over to the merchandise stand to buy an event t-shirt some time ago, and hadn't yet returned. Although they had planned a meeting place next to a particular pole, she couldn't even see the pole now, with the crowd later estimated between 450,000 and 500,000. She realized he had lost his family in the crowd.

Thinking she could seek help backstage, the very petite mom made her way through the crowd, which was "scary" at times, with people throwing water bottles. Her idea was to have someone make an announcement from the stage about a central spot where people could find their lost children of all ages, some of whom were standing alone in the backstage area. While there were several places designated by authorities to meet, Joyce knew these were spaced very far apart throughout the periphery of the crowd. The police rode around in "their little cars." Joyce wanted someone who had the clout to make the announcement to tell parents where to go to locate their children. She found the Chief of Police and they started arguing about the issue. The Chief refused to do what Joyce had suggested. The police drove her out of the backstage area warning her, "Don't come back." She found her daughter still at the blanket. Trying again, she talked to a woman who told her she could give her a backstage pass allowing Joyce to come and go in and out as she liked. Right before AC/DC, the second to last band, there was an announcement from the stage, but it was a different announcement, not the one Joyce had anticipated. She gave up.

While she was still in the backstage area, the Stones walked by. They said hi to everyone, about 25 people. She talked to Burton Cummings of The Who. Joyce was wearing little shorts and a tank stop and figured she fit in with the hangers-on backstage. She wanted to go back and find her daughter, thinking she might have to go over the fence, to bypass the huge crowd. This one police officer who had been nice earlier told her he could lift her over the tall fence. "He picked me up and dropped me on the other side," said Joyce. A very tall friend from childhood had come by and put Joyce's 16-year-old daughter on his shoulders, allowing her mom to see her above the crowd, when she returned. She tried to relax enough to enjoy the Stones at that point, saying, "They were great." She heard "Start Me Up", her favorite song. Following the fireworks closing out the Stones set, people started to leave. Joyce was still trying to get her hands on one of the little carts to travel around in, but couldn't. She walked to every designated meeting place on the edge of the crowd looking for Jason, except, as it turned out, the one where Jason had stood. She alternated between walking and running through the water bottles, and sitting down to rest. Finally she saw Jason walking down this long hallway. The three of them walked the long way to the car, where Joyce told the kids she would have to sleep for a couple of hours before she drove home. She was really tired, but just closed her eyes for twenty minutes. Her daughter had to be at work that morning, four hours away in Ottawa. In recounting her tale, Joyce compared the behavior of the Stones to another band:

The best part was seeing the Rolling Stones. AC/DC drove up in their limo, got onstage, got back in limo, and drove away...The Stones said hi to everyone.

She found the crowd "dangerous", and recalls that backstage, when trying to reach her goal, "They threw me out so many times, ten times".

Her son Jason, only fourteen, had a story to add to his mother's, from his perspective. He looked forward to seeing both bands, AC/DC and the Stones. He said they arrived so early, they ran in with the first twenty people to claim the "best place possible." When he left the blanket to go get a t-shirt, they had their blanket spread out, and no one was squishing them. Looking toward the path back, he noticed it had disappeared, along with the pole, the landmark that was supposed to guide them back together if anyone got lost or separated from the others. Jason switched between standing in one of the places for lost kids and walking into the crowd, at one point following a very large fellow who was trying to help someone else. Not wanting to tell anyone he was lost, thinking he'd make himself too vulnerable, he still "really had a good experience." In the heat, Jason fell asleep to be awakened to the chants of "woo woo" and fire bursting above him. That was "Sympathy for the Devil." When the place began emptying out, he started walking toward the exit, and his mom and sister were right there. He will never forget the experience, the beginning of his concert-going life, figuring if he could survive 500,000 people, he could handle anything. He loved "Sympathy" with the fireballs, calling it "celebratory song-playing."

Another benefit concert brought out Stonesdoug, this time in New York City in March 2006. Dedicated to fighting poverty in New York, The Robin Hood Foundation sponsored a private show for donors at the opulent Radio City Music Hall, the first time the Stones would play there. Stonesdoug has a knack for finding his place in the front, even without a ticket. During the acoustic set that replaced the B-stage numbers, played on a platform extending from the front of the main stage into the orchestra section, Doug *saw a guy going down there. I said I was with them...I told him as soon as your date gets back I'll move. I saw "As Tears Go By." That was the one my mom liked...*

Doug was about three feet away from Mick. He teared up as he watched and listened.

My new friend from Shidoobee, FarEastBam or Shigeo and I had met in the ticket line at the box office for the Radio City show, coincidentally, since I had helped him purchase his ticket online, when Ticketmaster gave him trouble. From Japan, FarEastBam often travels to the States on business. He recognized me in line right behind him, guessing it was me when we talked about how we got our tickets. We had separate seats at the show, both quite far back. Later I regretted not trying for a closer place down in the first mezzanine, the lowest of three balconies, lacking Doug's chutzpah to attempt to circumvent the tight security. Before the show a complimentary bar on each floor drew many patrons, some missing the opening notes of "Jumping Jack Flash," in no rush to sit down. Talking to people beforehand, I found people who had never seen the band. All ticketholders found a black t-shirt on their seat commemorating the occasion, a nice touch. On the front was a Stones tongue in the neon green of the Robin Hood logo, placed over a bulls-eye target in shades of gray. Playing primarily to men in white shirts arriving after work from their Wall Street jobs, Mick commented coquettishly, "I don't think I've ever played for such an affluent crowd!" The peak of the show for me was during "Sympathy" when both Mick and Keith climbed up the left and right projections built into the sides of the Art Deco hall. They unexpectedly turned these large, curved, wooden stairways into extensions of the stage. Keith kept going higher and higher, stopping right near my upper section, playing the whole time, and I couldn't help but scream in surprise and joy. At Radio City, built for musical performances, the sound was impeccable.

Shigeo and I had decided to meet back up and leave a little early before the end of the last encore, to try to catch a cab, with no success. As we walked further, we saw up close the four silver limos, one for each Rolling Stone, as they passed by. I waved but no one opened a darkened window. When we finally hailed a cab willing to pick us up, I gave him directions to where I was staying, but had made an error in telling the driver. All of a sudden, he stopped the cab, telling us to get out and walk because he didn't want to negotiate the one-way streets to circle back to the right path. Okay, we were only about halfway there, but thank you, sir! I love New York.

Live Filming: The Super Bowl Halftime and Scorsese's Shine a Light

A highlight for fans near Detroit, Michigan was participation in halftime at the Super Bowl XL performance of the Stones, like the SARS event, also in 2006. The Seahawks beat the Steelers 21-10, to win the National Football League championship, but the fans inside and outside of Ford Field concentrated on the fifteen-minute, three-song halftime show. Recruited by the Stones organization a month before 2,000 lucky fans filled the inside of a tongue-shaped structure forming the stage. This three-dimensional logo of the band was created especially for the event. Fans trained on how and when to carry in pieces of the stage and audience area and where to stand once they were in it. They didn't need coaching to act excited by the band's numbers. They were hidden at first, soon revealed as the pit audience, under the red, tongue-shaped cover.

A fan as a kid since the beginning, Detroitken knew he was going to go for the opportunity to see the band for free, in spite of an early requirement that you had to be under 45. He was 48, and "took offense" at that. The group leaders could be older. One guy in a leadership role had told his crew "if anyone was pissed off about that, lemme know." The officials later rescinded the ban against older people as long as they could do the running needed for the task. Other rules said everyone had to go to seven rehearsals in nine days, which eliminated many working people. Detroitken said in reality they had three rehearsals on Friday and Saturday, which meant people from Philly and other cities could have done it.

During practices, he met a few people he had known only online at Shidoobee. One person was Cindy P who was "a sweetheart," and there was another woman who "wanted to control everything." That person started to ask how they would find each other weeks before the show. She said she knew someone at Clear Channel and that she could get the schedule for the fans. As things turned out everyone in their twenty-person group got together on time, except that particular woman and "someone who will remain anonymous." Their job was to work with large gurneys that were 10 feet high and about 10-16 feet long. They had to roll them into place and connect them. Ken says the whole thing "was really cool." He has the vivid memory of being so close to the band during rehearsals, and for free.

Martin Scorsese wanted to make a contemporary concert film with The Rolling Stones. He and the band considered The Beacon Theater on the upper west side of New York City a perfect venue. Since the venue only held 2800 people between the floor, a loge, and two balconies above that, how to get in became a primary question for fans on the board. Of two shows in fall, 2006, one show would take place in honor of Bill Clinton's 60th birthday, with many of his cronies and friends attending. Ever the politician the former President shook hands with people who had lined up outside the Beacon. Containing much of the footage used in the final film called *Shine a Light*, the second night was filled with fans that secured tickets, costing only 35 dollars face value for balcony seats. Those seats went very quickly. Before the tickets went on sale for the Beacon, an enterprising member of the Undercover fan group organized a "buying circle." People would volunteer to work online when the tickets first appeared, using each other's charge cards to buy tickets. Typically when tickets are scarce, they had most luck buying one or at the most two at a time.

One other method of getting in was to successfully pass the audition for the "extras" cast to fill in the audience downstairs. Putting out a call through Shidoobee's Stonesdoug, the casting director asked for headshots through email so she could select extras for the audience. Many of us, including me, didn't make the cut. We were too old, too ugly, or somehow didn't fit the image she was seeking of a Stones fan appropriate for the film. One person was turned down for wearing too many items with Stones logos or tongues. Meanwhile fans on IORR complained that they didn't have the opportunity to audition. Their turn came later on for the 50 and Counting Tour when fans there in select cities such as London, New York and Los Angeles could try out for the video that the Stones showed before every show. Those were solo spots with clips of individual fans including some celebrities to give brief impressions of the band. Along with a few others from IORR, wearing her black-rimmed glasses, Thru and Thru of Shidoobee and IORR secured a short spot in the introductory movie. Auditioning in L.A., she exclaimed on film, "Oh, my god, who are these guys?" in apparent response to a question on how she felt when she first heard them. She was shocked that she made the final cut, given how the questions were phrased and her off-the-cuff answers.

A third method of obtaining a seat for the Beacon, or in this case, a pair of them was to win an essay contest sponsored by rollingstones.com. The subject to write about was "Why should The Rolling Stones Fan Club send you to the Beacon Theatre?" VirginiaJagger won seats to the second show when she wrote that she was turning 60 soon, just like Bill Clinton, and, like him, would very much appreciate celebrating her birthday in the presence of The Rolling Stones. With many fans, Virginia believes that with all the entries received, the Stones organization probably just chose the winners by lottery, by chance. Not knowing, but from seeing just a few entries, I disagree, thinking they went for depth of excitement, and colorful expression of feelings, preferring brevity to wordiness.

You Get What You Need

People who couldn't get tickets were devastated. A few paid several hundred dollars to scalpers. Those who were officially in the house felt happy and lucky. A glitch came when the second show was postponed a day from Oct. 31 to Nov. 1 probably due to the strain on Mick's voice from practice and the first Beacon show on Oct. 29. The band had postponed the earlier Atlantic City show that came too close to rehearsals and filming dates. Some fans from out of state had to go back to work and couldn't attend the new date at the Beacon. Others changed flights and hotel reservations, feeling glad that they could. At first the extras were told they could bring friends along for a rehearsal between shows but because of the changed date, those plans were scratched for retaining only the original extras. A very few of the people cast from Shidoobee such as Drake and Debi took their places alongside the young models hired to pack the front, and the others sat elsewhere. Featured in an article in The New Yorker about the filming, Debi stood right in front of Keith, interacting with him for much of the show. She and the other extras in the cast were paid 75 dollars for their "work," a fantasy come true for diehard fans.

Before the second show, a few fans scheduled for the rehearsal at schoolhouse PS 87 near the theater informed their friend cut from the amended extras list that they could join in, that spaces had opened up. They were told to bring two forms of ID and they would take a shuttle to the venue after they had signed in. They finished all the protocol, receiving their all-important bracelets for admission. After entering the Beacon with their wristbands, the same group of Shidoobees soon found an unwelcome reception. They were asked to get out, even though they had already found their seats. The staff member cut their bracelets off, escorting them to the door. Mickgrrl found the disappointment and frustration monumental: "We were so excited, and they came up to us and told us we had to leave. We're like, 'What do you mean?'" They were told that they had mistakenly been allowed entrance. Everyone except one guy who had gone to the bathroom, staying there until he thought the coast was clear was kicked out. One person from the group remained undetected. Suspecting what was going on, this guy chose an apropos moment to visit the men's room, staying there until he thought the coast was clear. He found a seat to watch the show after his friends were ejected. Most who didn't get in were successful in seeing the show two nights later by finding and a ticket, often from scalpers who could charge near five figures apiece for this theater show.

The second show contained most all of the footage used in the film, other than a few minutes introducing former President Clinton from the first night. The hardcore fans filling the audience sang along to every song. Even though most of us were seated too far up in the stands to show up in the film, we had a great time, knowing we made it in the room. Everyone with tickets in the first balcony, behind me in the second balcony, and below me in the loge, stood up for most or all of the show. Later I learned that a few people had paid an usher to make their way onto the floor of the orchestra, to occupy empty seats in the back rows. One fan, not alone, complained loudly in the lobby about how the director didn't treat the real fans too well. To me, it was a film project rather than purely a Rolling Stones show, the special theater dates mounted for the movie, and I was glad to be there. That night I met a man standing behind me, a Mick Jagger look-a-like, a very nice guy. A woman near me asked to have a photo taken with him, in his black t-shirt with the Omega circa Mick's stage outfit in 1969. He went on to perform with the tribute band "The Glimmer Twins," taking the front man's role.

Maysles' Film Footage from 1969

Another special event took place in 2007 when a Shidoobee close to him talked to Albert Maysles, the surviving half of the fraternal duo who filmed the Altamont concert for the documentary Gimme Shelter (1970). They discussed the possibility of a fundraiser for his non-profit organization, the Maysles Institute. With michelejagger's help, Stonesdoug organized a small gathering in New York for fans to meet

Albert and watch some unreleased film from the shows at Madison Square Garden. The band had played The Garden in New York City in 1969 over Thanksgiving weekend, a week before Altamont. The co-director of *Gimme Shelter* spliced footage from those shows they had recorded into their film. Some of the music from those concerts is featured on 1969's live album *Get Yer Ya-Ya's Out!* Using the name of the album, Maysles and others made the footage into a 27-minute film released in 2009.

Conclusions

In the imagined contest for the greatest rock and roll band of all time, The Rolling Stones are virtually peerless in their longevity and appeal onstage. The live shows are at the heart of the hardcore fan's love for the band. A fan from Sarasota, Florida with his own weekly radio show "Ripper's Rarities" compares The Stones to The Beatles in their early years: "The Stones were the greatest live band." Singling out the 1973 bootleg *The Brussels Affair,* Ripper says he had never heard a live album better than that, adding, "The Stones could release every live show they've ever done." While "representing their generation better than anyone," The Beatles stopped touring in 1966. "The Beatles were a studio band." Performances of the two bands in the later 60s and early 70s were

> *not just a concert for us, they were leading the culture... In the 70s, it was an event, but they were in their prime, at the peak of their popularity. The Stones are in town! It was like a world heavyweight fight.*

A writer in *The Rolling Stones and Philosophy* said that no matter how many times you've heard a song, the recorded version is just "a template" for how the band might play it during any particular gig (Merklinger, 2012, p. 82). Fans like to notice the details within the moment-to-moment playing in the space for improvisation that the songs provide. Ugotthesilver "got the touring bug" going to all three shows at Madison Square Garden in January 1998. He had the chance to see how they really operated as a band. He mused that even if "you know what the set list may be...you never know how they will play it" because a song may sound different than it did two days earlier. From the rarely played tunes to the most common warhorses of the set, the music can sometimes result in either "total disaster" or "rock'n'roll perfection," says Merklinger, the latter like the two shows recorded in Brussels. Along with complaining online about the similarity of set lists within a tour, hard core fans who have gone to many shows talk about the very best versions of songs they have heard live, comparing the expressiveness and the technique, and the enthusiasm of band members and audiences.

Aside from supplying the soundtracks of their lives, the band's tours provide opportunities for adventures before, during, and after the shows that stick in a fan's mind among the best nights of their lives. The band's powerfully sensual music and memorable lyrics combine with its charismatic, identifiable personalities and the spectacle of the costumes, the venue and the stage setting to tell an affecting theatrical story. Comingling with those facets of The Rolling Stones' performances of five plus decades are the friendships among fans, old and new, and for some, the drugs and alcohol to make indelible memories.

CHAPTER SIX:

"ROCKS OFF: THE TONGUE PIT EXPERIENCE ON THE *50 AND COUNTING* TOUR"

"I've been very close to the Stones number of times, but this time, it really felt like we hit the jackpot." (Johnny Otiac)

Celebrating the 50th Anniversary: Would It Happen?

The uncertain future as a band post-2007 seemed to center around the relationship of Mick and Keith, and Keith's health. Three of the four central members had played the occasional gig, whereas Keith had not, during the interim of four or five years. Every time rumors surfaced of a new tour, nothing happened. Then finally Keith appeared at the Apollo in February 2012 at the Hubert Sumlin tribute. Playing with a number of musicians outside the band, he showed he still had the chops to perform in public. On the other hand, the controversy from Keith's autobiography *Life* appeared, raising the issue of Keith's much-publicized "tiny todger" remark. Keith negatively characterized Mick's sexual attributes, if not his sexual prowess per se. How bothered was Mick by Keith's comment? Supposedly, Keith had offered the manuscript to Mick to read, but either he had overlooked the comment or it had not bothered him until spread throughout the media worldwide. On Shidoobee, a fan kept posting against the possibility of a tour, saying, "It's over" with the trademark sign™. Yes, it did seem over, until it wasn't.

An apology from Keith to Mick sparked the steps to spur the shows into fruition. The band named the tour *50 and Counting,* although Mick had long maintained his disdain for official anniversaries. The tour title commemorated the fifty years that had passed since the band formed to play their first gig in 1962. Sprinkled in at the start of each leg were rehearsals and two small shows in Paris, one rehearsal opened to thirty lucky fans standing outside, and then a club show at the Echoplex in LA for fans picked in a lottery among the hopefuls lined up to get in. They also did a short set at Madison Square Garden on 12-12-12 for a benefit for Hurricane Sandy victims.

The band rolled out their arena shows in phases, first in late 2012, doing two shows at the London O2 venue, with original bassist Bill Wyman performing on two songs. Mick Taylor also rejoined as a guest player. They continued with three shows in the greater New York area, one night in Brooklyn, and two shows in Newark, the second filmed for a pay-for-view television audience. After the success of these concerts, the band scheduled a group of shows in 2013, first in the U.S., primarily on the two coasts, plus Chicago. They returned to London that summer for two outdoor shows at Hyde Park, and finally, at Glastonbury, their first time at the annual UK festival. In a move applauded by many hardcore fans, Mick Taylor stayed with the band, typically playing on two songs, but varying from one to four per show for nearly the entire run. The indoor arena shows included special guests playing, singing or both on one number with the band, rather than an opening act.

After a description of the new stage with the pit, fans discuss how they came to buy the expensive pit tickets and their reactions to being so close to the band. People selected to turn in their "cheap" 85.00 tickets for pit tickets also talk about what they experienced. Finally, the idea of "role embracement" (Goffman, 1961) makes sociological sense out of the avid fan participation to apply to hardcore followers of any band or celebrity, or committed practitioners of any leisure time pursuit.

The New Stage: The Tongue Pit

For the early indoor portion of their *50 and Counting* tour in London and the States, the Stones took away the B-stage and walkway to replace it with standing room only in "the tongue pit" in front of the stage. The novelty of a tongue-shaped area was enhanced by the ramp outlining the lower lip surrounding the tongue pit, forming a narrow path for Mick, and occasionally for Keith and Ronnie to walk around. The lip ramp stood between the standing fans in the tongue pit and the other fans with seats on the floor or on the lower sides. Shaped and colored like an upper lip and teeth, a giant balloon mounted directly above the stage completed the tongue logo of the band, complementing the pit and the ramp.

Other than insiders with special access, two types of situations allowed entrance to the pit. First, people willing to pay 1500 dollars or so in the U.S gained entrance, with the so-called VIP Pit package. London fans paid about half that if for non-VIP tickets, an option available at the O2 and later at outdoor European shows. VIP status entitled ticket-holders early admission to the pit, guaranteeing a spot in the first rows for people lining up early enough. The second and much rarer method started in 2013 was to bet on the chance to have your relatively cheap 85-dollar "mystery" or "lottery" tickets switched to a pit location when you picked them up before the show. Not a bad investment, with the full price almost eighteen times the 85 dollars.

With the traditional front rows of the floor pushed back to make room for the pit, the front floor as well as the back pit had a great view of Mick and the boys as they circled the rim of the pit area, the bottom of the tongue-shaped pit. At Montreal's show one fan estimated that Mick came around for five or six songs, Ronnie, for three and Keith for two. At some point in the tour Mick started slapping hands of the people in the front areas. He treated IORR's leader Bjornulf to a full handshake at a west coast show, after seeing and hearing him in the pit several times in a row.

Making the Decision to Buy Pit Tickets

People decided to spring for the "pit tix" for a variety of reasons, ranging from the mundane to the special situation. Once fans saw that the whole pit area replaced the seats that were near the front, approximately the closest twenty rows or so, they knew the pit was the ideal place to be. If a fan wanted to stand up through the whole concert, the decision became more about justifying the expense, whether just to themselves or to others in their lives. One young fan admitted to lying to his mother and his girlfriend about the ticket cost because they would be angry. They already think he's "crazy" for spending too much money on the band.

After noting that people have called her "a sucker" and that she's been told to "get a f'ing life," Betsy, a compact blonde with curly hair and glasses, explains her decision, related to her life style:

As for why the pit, I was on the floor for both shows in NJ last December, the 2nd one I was on the rail just outside the pit. And yes, I really wanted in. But it's more than just "I want I want I want."

I don't drive a fancy car. I don't wear fancy clothes. I don't live in a mini-mansion. My main entertainment expenses in my life are soccer dues for the teams I play on and then maybe going out to dinner or a movie from time to time. And buying Rolling Stones tickets every 5 years or so.

I identify with what she says here, in that my own lifestyle is not extravagant. In the pit, others told me similar stories about how they don't have big houses, or own boats, and didn't ordinarily take expensive vacations.

Betsy bought two pit tickets for herself and her husband for Las Vegas, so they could spend a three-day weekend together. For her, creating mutual memories is a crucial part of her relationship.

...I know that he and I will have an amazing time, enjoy ourselves...and have a memory that lasts us a lifetime. We talk, to this day, about certain shows we've been to together and the wonderful bits and pieces of those shows, the experiences we had. To me, it's priceless to build those memories and I'm finally making enough money so I can do it and not take 6 months to pay it off.

She will also go to Philly with floor tickets, because "the memories" she'll have of the two shows, even alone, without her "best friend" husband, for her, "are worth the cash."

Coming in from Japan, FarEastBam reasons that the band does not have too many years left to tour. He says "I think, we cannot see their show many times from now on. So I go to America with much effort..." Like other lucky fans, he has sat close to the stage before, at least once in the "front row," and he really "wants to see" them up there again, from the best possible spot.

A tall, silver-haired gentleman from California, Wembley met his blonde, bespectacled wife Diane in 2000 at a Shidoobee gathering in Wildwood, New Jersey. He declined Diane's offer to get him a pit ticket when she and a friend decided to buy them. "I said no--it just seemed way to much money for the perceived experience." He had already spent loads of cash on tickets for shows in Brooklyn and Newark the year before. He had also been to theater shows in 2002-2003 at the Boston Orpheum, the New York Roseland and the Vredenburg, Utrecht. He didn't see how the pit could beat those small venues. Even though she was with him at those shows, Wembley says, "Obviously," Diane and her friend "have different views on the subject."

Diane added detail, giving two reasons for wanting pit tix, first the "unique concept of the tongue pit." She and Wembley had the special onstage balcony seats built into the stage above and behind the band for the last PacBell show in San Francisco on *A Bigger Band* tour. She enjoyed the view from that vantage point, "very different and fun to do." Second, she is "frustrated " with the way on-sale tickets are distributed now. It used to be you could secure front row seats or close to that if you got online early.

> *Even if you manage to sign on first thing for on sale, there is no chance to get anything close to front row seats. Those are all withheld for VIPs or seem to wind up in ticket brokers' hands. Didn't used to be that way. We got front row Oakland in 2002 online...*

If you want front row now, says Diane, you're going to have to pay "inflated scalper prices similar to pit prices, or worse. In which case, getting pit directly seems more worthwhile." On the other side, Wembley notes that both he and Diane "seemed to have become addicted to the $85 mystery tix."

Growing up in Utah, in Salt Lake City, icirider is a lifelong fan, but never had a chance to see a Stones concert until the *Voodoo Lounge* tour. He paid for a seat in the first six rows, spoiling himself then and thereafter, he says. Echoing Betsy, he and his live-in girlfriend of ten years "both make decent livings, but are not wealthy by any means." She didn't want to travel outside of their home area in the northwest U.S., so icirider decided on Vegas by himself because "it was on a Saturday, and I wouldn't need to take any time off work, and it's a relatively short flight from Portland." He figured if his girlfriend had wanted to go, they'd be paying $1500 for two lower bowl tickets anyway. Also despite the cost, he thinks Las Vegas on *50 and Counting* might be the last show he sees.

You Get What You Need

I'm only going to one show. I see this as most likely my "farewell" to my favorite live band of all time, and I want to go out with a bang. I do admit to some anger over the vulgar pricing and I think that they are "taking liberties" with their longstanding fans. But what are you gonna do?

Among the younger crowd of fans, there are those dying to see more shows, with at least as much fervor as the older people. Joanne, in her early thirties, and benstones, in his twenties, describe their motives. "Those of us like myself who are younger," says Joanne, have seen the Stones infrequently up until now, because of their age, and not having the funds to travel before. She's gone to their concerts only "a handful of times" since her first show in '89, even though she's followed them from the age of eleven.

She's saved her money for two years, thinking, with icirider, that this "is probably the last time" she will see them. She plans to get in the front row of the pit, for a "once in a lifetime opportunity" to see them up close in Chicago where she lives.

I am going to be in the front of that Pit against the rails if it kills me. I sincerely hope they didn't sell a lot of VIP packages so that I can ensure I'm in the front.... I want to be FIRST IN LINE like Riff Randell in Rock 'N Roll High School.

Taking no chances she arrived very early, at 1 p.m. finding herself behind several other people there before her. She sat on her "little camping chair" and talked to the people around her. If the Stones never tour again, she can say she saw them the last time around and from the front row center, achieving her goal.

Living in Mexico now, of French background, twenty-three year old benstones stresses that he "can't enjoy a show...being seated." He understands that not everyone can stand up for more than two hours, "but I am young and I need to move," he says. He wants to stand very near the stage, so he can "jump" with his "arms pointed" toward the band:

I LOVE to be close to the band. I always arrive early to be in the front row. I love when Keith looks at me. It happened 4 or 5 times during my 13 Stones shows. Lisa sent me three kisses too.

He wants to demonstrate his allegiance to the band, especially to older fans,

to prove to the other fans that ME TOO, I am a fan of the Rolling Stones. I am proud to be 23 and to be a Stones fan. Some people when they don't know me think that I am not a fan, that I am just going to my first show. No, I want to show them that we can be young and crazy about the Stones.

A pit ticket guarantees his standing spot up front where he is free to dance about and interact with the band, and it gives him maximum visibility within the crowd.

A story both sad and happy, starts with a daughter who went with her dad to over twenty Rolling Stones shows, the last in 2006 at the MGM Grand the night Mick's father had died in London soon after Mick left for Las Vegas. Three years later, her own father went into cardiac arrest suddenly, passing away when he was only 51, and she was 23. A dietician, she decided to specialize in cardiology after that. Here known only as an anonymous fan at her request, the daughter had a headstone made up for her dad, posting a picture on a fan board.

There is a Stones tongue instead of a dash between his two dates, and the lyrics "you can't always get what you want, but if you try sometimes, you just might find, you get what you need." I obviously didn't want him to die so young, but I needed to have him in my life and I'm so lucky I did. He was really the best and I miss him every day.

The loving daughter ended up buying pit seats for several shows, bringing photos of the headstones with notes to the Stones on the back. She "paper-airplaned" a bunch of them onto the stage, and "Keith actually picked one up and put it in his back pocket. I know my Dad would have loved that." She gave one to Keith's daughter Alex too, who is exactly her age.

So there has been a lot of strange overlap and opportunities to include my Dad that would not have happened if I wasn't as close as the pit allowed for.

She remembers how her dad always liked to sit next to the catwalk, to be as close as possible when they walked by. She knows he "would have gone absolutely crazy in the pit." She felt being at the shows was "the closest thing to being with her dad", which was great, and yet she still couldn't help crying every time during "You Can't Always Get What You Want."

The daughter received a surprise proposal during the Las Vegas show in the pit. I was standing in front of her fiancé when he told some of us he was going to propose to his girlfriend, asking another fan to take their picture. They had been dating for eight years, but she was resistant to getting married. She says, "Of course, I accepted what was really the perfect proposal." She has decided to take a break for herself though, feeling uncertain about the lifetime commitment after all the change she went through in the last few years.

A fan from Las Vegas who went to shows in London and the States in 2012 and 2013, IGTBA ("It's good to be anywhere") noted that when the new arena layout came out, no one knew for sure if the pit was the best place to see the shows or not. He decided to go for a VIP pit ticket for the second London show, while snagging a Facebook single in the sixth row on the floor, Ronnie's side, for the initial concert. Security at the O2 allowed fans to stand a couple of people deep at the rail on the floor. While standing at the rail, IGTBA says,

It immediately became apparent to me that the pit was the better place to be - at least for me. It is crowded at the front of the pit - and you need to be there a long time before the concert starts and stay there - but it's super to be just a few feet away from the band members during most of the concert

He found out from the shows that the front of the pit is much closer than the front row on the floor, except for the times when they go out on the walkway to the "tip" of the tongue.

For the 2013 tour, IGTBA would have purchased VIP pit tickets for multiple shows, but he became aggravated at what the promoters did for the first Hyde Park London sale. He and others from the fan boards had bought the GA (General Admission) Tier I tickets, top price and hard to get, with advertised "access to the area directly in front of the stage." The next day that area was moved to the left side, with GA3s, the lowest priced GAs moved to the space provided in front. When angry people complained online at IORR, and directly to AEG, the promoters, they were told they could have refunds, if desired. In protest of the new seating plan, IGBTA ended up buying just one pit seat for Las Vegas where he lived, and the 85-dollar mystery tickets for some other shows.

Ellen (ellip) noticed that every other seat seemed "way too far away" after she saw photos of the pit from shows before Oakland. Someone from Shidoobee had put up these "pit pics", saying the experience was worth the expense. She used money from her entertainment budget to pay for the "ridiculously expensive" tickets because she needed to be in the front row, in front of Keith. Ellen explained:

I wanted to say Thanks and I wanted to say Goodbye to a group of guys whose music I have treasured for decades and who have

brought me joy and laughter and happiness like no one else in my entire life.

Ellen carefully planned her strategy to make sure she attained her objective: standing in the front row in the pit.

For me, it was a combination of reasons stated here--wanting to be close, and wanting to say goodbye, knowing this run was among the last series of shows the band would perform. I ended up swept away, buying a pit for the first Newark show, and then for Las Vegas, where I've enjoyed shows at the MGM Grand since the *Voodoo Lounge* tour. I figured Las Vegas pit tix would disappear quickly, so that one was a no-brainer, and after Newark, a must-see spot.

To cut the cost, I tried for a less expensive non-VIP pit on Facebook, but the very few available tickets vanished almost immediately. For the London O2 shows that sparked off the tour, some fans from IORR scored "regular" non-VIP tickets for less than half the price of the standard VIP pit tickets in the U.S. Word on the boards implied that if you had an in with Shelley Lazar of the band's organization, she could sell you pits for two-thirds of the regular stateside price. To wait for the chance that pit tix would go for less was not an option for most travellers, and the secondary market, including ebay showed prices way up from face value.

Waiting, Entering, and Securing a Place in the Pit

In England, the pit tickets were sold as both VIP packages and non-VIP tickets, without any extras. The VIPS in London had a dinner before the show, whereas in the U.S., for some shows, patrons who wanted close seats on the floor could buy a package that included dinner. U.S. pit patrons, however, would just receive a package with a program, a badge, and a stadium-size wool red blanket with a large tongue on the front. The pit package would also provide the purchaser with early entry in comparison to the rare Facebook ticket-holder, along with a number of mystery ticket buyers who got lucky at the arena shows in the spring and summer of 2013.

In London, The Beast had expected the VIPS to have their own gold circle in the very front of the pit at the first show at the O2, the kick-off, but to her surprise, she "ran in there to find the rail waiting" for her. She said the VIPS, the majority of ticket-holders for the pit, didn't come in until later, in a group, "by which time all the rail space had gone." Kindly advising me on what to do, knowing that each venue may differ, Beast said if I want to be at the rail I should head straight for it when the doors opened. If she were not at the rail, she would probably choose to be at the side by the rim.

How Beast and her friend attained the front row spots was first making sure she was near the front of the queue in the standing line outside. They sat in the bar outside the entrance before that, watching for when the queue began forming, as it turns out, only "shortly before the doors opened." Then after getting her wristband, Beast made a mad dash for the pit:

> *...I ran up the stairs instead of using the escalator and must have been one of the first 15-20 people in there. There was no crush, you could leave to go to the bathroom or bar (though I only did that before showtime) and it all seemed to be very civilized, with plenty of room.*

For the second show, Beast and her friend obtained pit tix at the last minute. She still made it to her spot, although the process had changed a bit. You had to queue up again at the roped off doors, after you either ran up the stairs, Beast's method, or rode the escalator. Then a security guard told the waiting fans that once the inside doors opened you had to walk, not run down to the floor. This time a set of doors, on the other side swung open, letting the people there in first, until Beast pointed out to her usher that he needed to open their doors too. That slight delay still gave Beast time to run over to reach her previous place at the rail. She says "luckily for us," not everyone wanted to be at the front, some preferring to stand further back or next to the outer rim.

At the beginning of the tour, it appeared that fewer seats were put up for sale for the pit, or fewer actually sold, anyway, before the 85-dollar tickets were introduced. Pit areas from early shows, the two in London, and Brooklyn through at least the first Newark show held a relatively small number of people, allowing for much movement throughout the show, for people who wanted to switch viewing spots. Past the first ten or twelve rows of the pit, space appeared plentiful, looking at the photos from those venues. The outer rim of the tongue that encircled the pit space was not used much by the band at the beginning, and when it was, it was almost always Mick who walked along it. From Beast's observation, situated in the front row just to the left of Mick's microphone, "even he didn't go the whole way around too often. But I had such a marvelous vantage point that my eyes stayed glued to the stage the whole time."

As the tour went on, people at the sides and back of the pit saw close-up views of Keith and Ronnie at select times, and Mick quite frequently. Mick became more comfortable there, often covering the whole rim in both directions, stopping to dance in place at a few intervals in many songs. Those at the front typically watched the rest of the band while Mick took off to walk, skip, or even run the rim. This movement gave the fans in seats at the sides and the front floor a close-up look at the front man and once in a while, the two guitarists, akin to the B-stage of other shows, but lasting throughout the show, and without Charlie or Chuck.

Leaving the VIP dinner early before the second London show, IGTBA says he skipped dessert to go into the pit early. Even so, he was not able to make the rail, but he was "standing on the rail grating with only one row of people" in front of him. He planned to stay in place for the first two/thirds of the concert, and then "wander around the pit for the rest." That worked for him toward the last part of the show, which he spent in the back half of the pit. There it was "uncrowded, except immediately next to the walkway," a more relaxed atmosphere than at the front.

Uh-huh uh huh, whose real name is B H McCarthy, purchased a pit for the second Newark show, the pay-per-view. He went to the show by himself, and stood in line from 2 p.m. onward, to end up front and center in the pit. He also bought a pit for the Oakland show and convinced his friend to join him for "an unbelievable experience...priceless." They planned to take the BART train in, and wait in line while "tag team tailgating" with Shidoobees.

In Chicago, Joanne arrived at about 2 p.m. to secure her place, 6th or 8th from the beginning of the line that she found out started an hour earlier. She began to chat with those around her, learning that the guy behind her was from Brazil. She met a young man in his twenties who "looked more like 16, from France." He had been to all three shows in LA, and he was seeing all three in Chicago. When Jo asked him how he could do that, he told her "his mother gave him the money."

After a while, Uma, the staff person came out, and told Joanne's boyfriend not to worry about getting his pair of 85-dollar tickets, even though Joanne had to stand in line for the pit. Joanne stood in two lines, first to get the wristband, and then back outside to wait again. She said staff let them in about 5:45 to line up again before walking them down the stairs and into the pit. At that moment, she noticed, how "It is so surreal looking around and nobody else is in the venue." She stood exactly front row center, directly "in front of the teleprompter" used by Mick during the show. She talked to several "Stones virgins" around her in the pit while "some guys" were buying her beers, having much fun while waiting for the band to come on.

Fretting about how she would make it to the front at Oakland, Ellen (ellip) looked everywhere online for what time the doors would open. One rumor had it that if you tried to line up before 5 or 6 p.m. management would turn you away. Ellen figured it would take longer than that before show time "with all the people they had to process". She decided to start waiting at 1 p.m., before the cars began to line up to enter parking lots that opened at 3 p.m. She purposely didn't share her plan online. Using BART, she arrived first in line at the entrance at 12:55. She explained:

> *It was a GA meritocracy and I was willing to do whatever it took to get the spot I wanted...*

> *One fan wandered by about 10 minutes later to chat, but left as he was a pit veteran. It was not critical for him to be at the rail, and he was just out for a stroll at his hotel.*

Two other females joined her in a little while, and by 4 p.m., there were still fewer than twenty fans in line. Spending six hours in line together, "we were quite friendly", and "all of us made it to the front row and I got the exact spot I wanted." By 6 p.m., however, there were hundreds of people, some confused about whether or not they were in the right line, now composed of "VIP pit people, GA Pit and Hospitality Tickets and a few lost 85 souls", says Ellen.

In Las Vegas for her first pit show, nursejane and I teamed up for a place in line. She called me early, shortly past noon, saying a line to the pit had formed. She had an appointment to get her hair done in the hotel, and would join me when she was done. I went downstairs from my conveniently located room at the MGM, bought well ahead of time at a reasonable rate, to see that a long line was indeed waiting, but not for entry to the auditorium. They wanted merchandise, t-shirts and other paraphernalia related to the show. A few people sat near a door, and after finding out that they held pit tickets, I decided to join them, rather than going back up to the room. They asked me how many people I was with, and I told them only one.

Talking to those in line, I met a mother and a daughter directly behind me. The 18-year-old daughter told me that she had found the Stones music online, just by looking around for music and to see who was hanging out in different spaces online. Her mom was somewhat of a fan, but liked a number of bands equally as well. A father I had hung out with in line along with his daughter at the first Newark show spotted me and we hugged like long-lost friends. Unlike the daughter in line here, his 19-year-old offspring had picked up her interest in the band from her father's passion. Once in a while someone yelled "Shidoobee," and then others of us would answer "Shidoobee," and sometimes find each other in the line or walking by. A married couple in front of me, Sharon and Bob, had brought their three kids, ranging in age from teen-aged to a 30 years old plus one or two of their children's friends.

Waiting inside the MGM Grand Hotel was nice, a breeze in comparison to Newark, where we all waited outdoors in the damp, chilly December air for a few hours. At the MGM, you could buy food and drinks nearby while waiting too, as people kept your place in line. You could also leave the pit area for bathroom or refreshment breaks and re-enter easily, showing the wristband. The only tense time came in the line during the waiting process when a set of inner doors opened to go closer to the audience area, and for some reason, security formed another line with people from the back who had arrived much later. A young couple in front of that second line had already aggressively pushed ahead and seemed determined to blend in with the front of our line, trying to convince the ushers to merge the two lines. Nursejane was having none of that and expressed her feelings out loud. A few of us gave a heads up to a large male usher who didn't seem to care at all, and also spoke with a young female usher who acted confused and kept claiming she didn't know anything. Finally, while going to another area to wait further, behind yet another set of doors, the two lines went back to one, in the same order as before.

When they let us in, I was momentarily blinded by the darkness and became disoriented, walking past my target, until I heard Jane calling me over to where she was at the front rail. Settling in, I was happy having people to chat with who were huge fans, and yet peaceful, in contrast to a person at my other front pit experience, several months earlier. Sandwiched between nursejane, my tall assertive friend with her freshly coiffed hair on my right, and Bob directly to my left with his tribe of six or so, I had a formidable barrier against would-be encroachers to our space, plus two calm and courteous co-watchers, one on each side. Before the show began, I asked Bob how big a fan of the band his wife Sharon was. Bob told me that if Sharon wasn't big into the Stones, no way would they have lasted. Over the years, he would take the women he was dating on a test run to a Rolling Stones show to see how they responded before deciding whether to continue or to stop the relationship. A lukewarm or negative reaction by his date meant Bob was outta there.

Later on we heard about a commotion in the pit that turned out to be triggered by the same belligerent couple from the second line, now pushing toward the front row. A fan from Shidoobee was on crutches a few rows from the stage. When the two attempted to pass by him, he grabbed the man's arm, pulled him back, and they exchanged a few words, before the man disappeared back into the crowd. Soon two security guards called our Shidoobee friend out from the pit area, relaying the news that the aggressive fan had accused the Shidoobee on crutches of throwing him to the ground. This "assault" charge was jeopardizing his chances of staying at the show. The Shidoobee told security to go into the pit crowd to ask people if they would confirm his side of the story. After what seemed like an eternity, the guards told him he was allowed to return. He didn't know how he could negotiate his way toward the front to his former spot where his girlfriend, now wife, had stayed. To his surprise and joy, people had cleared a path for him in the packed pit, and were cheering him on his return.

In Toronto for a pit seat, nursejane found herself first in line in the freezing rain, joined by about fifty people for 90 minutes before the outside doors opened. She snagged the same spot in the pit as she had at the MGM Grand, in front and a little to the right of center, so she could watch Keith up close. She had a worse experience during this show with one person next to her who kept shoving her and interjecting loud comments during the show. We agreed that having someone you already know next to you, in this case, each other, made for a much better time, even if the band was just as good as before, if not better. Jane and I had met online at Shidoobee and then connected at breakfast in the Holiday Inn on the day of the first Newark show. As she did in Las Vegas, in Toronto, nursejane managed to charm the evening's set list from a willing security guard.

My pit location in Newark, five months before at the first U.S. show of *50 and Counting* was the same as in Las Vegas, to the right of Mick's microphone, on the rail. However, I failed to pay enough attention to who wound up on either side of me among the various people in line. On my right was a great guy in his 50's, very mild-mannered, who asked me if I wanted anything from concessions. He brought me a chocolate chip cookie that hit the spot. I didn't want to drink much at all. Once we made it inside, most of us toward the front of the line had made a run to the bathroom before we went down into the Barclay Center pit. On the other side of me was a young man brandishing a sign that said, "Charlie, give me your stick!" Early on, he kept shouting into the crowd "I'm not gay!" to dissuade any lewd interpretations of his printed words. This fan alternated between jumping up and down with the sign and taking pics with his phone held in the air. My view was blocked at times with his antics. At one point late in the show, Mick acknowledged the fellow's sign, and the young man's face showed joyous relief. Mick rolled his eyes in my direction. I did the same back.

Known as Still a Fool, Charles describes the wait for the Chicago shows in two parts. He says you "get there around 5, wait in line for a while, and then wait in the pit for a while longer." Even though the pit was more crowded for both Chicago shows in the United Center than for Barclays in Brooklyn, the fans, "being mature, did not push and were respectful." He remarks that the "social aspect" of the pit is unusual because of the long wait together in line.

> *You get to talk to a lot of people who share the love of the Rolling Stones with you. I met some really nice people at both shows. Of the dozens of other Stones shows I've seen, I don't remember meeting anyone (Shidoobee gatherings aside.)*

In lines both outdoors and indoors in different cities, Charles continues,

> *On line outside I spoke to a woman I'd met in Brooklyn, and once inside saw a guy I had talked to in Chicago so it really is quite a social place as I mentioned before.*

Charles found the wait for the pit "highly worth it," to be so close to the action and see the expressions on band members' faces.

In comparing his pit experiences, Charles mentioned how at Philly 2, fewer people were waiting for the early VIP access than in Brooklyn and Chicago. "We didn't show up especially early and were still able to secure a spot touching the security barrier" on Keith's side, in contrast to standing behind two rows of people in the pit at the other venues. He saw that, nonetheless, the show seemed much more crowded by the time the show started. This could mean that the organizers turned many more 85 tickets into pit spots, or possibly that people crashed the pit. In going to several shows, I gathered that fans at certain venues such as Las Vegas had bought more of the VIP tix at face value or higher, limiting the proportion of mystery tix designated for pits. More fans in the Philly area, for example, may have balked at the full-priced pit tix, allowing a higher percentage of the audience in who held mystery tix. Perhaps too, as time went by, the number of pit entries permitted or the pit capacity itself was increased by the particular venue, for maximum availability of spots. More people inside the pit meant reduced room for individuals to stand and move around, even toward the middle and back areas.

Thinking he might share the line to the pit with bankers and traders, benstones was surprised that most of the people were "huge fans" like him, "crazy fans" who bought the tickets they really wanted, despite the expense. Ben lies to both his mum and girlfriend about the price of the tickets, because he knows they'd be angry with him for spending so much. Ben is not alone in his deception, hiding the cost from friends and family. I know that because I usually tell people, especially the non-fans, that I don't want to talk about specific prices. Sometimes they insist on taking a guess or two, asking, for example, "Is it more than 300 dollars?" I say "Uh-huh," and close down the conversation while they shake their heads in disbelief. Other fans have close associates who accept their passion for the band, from listening habits to collecting bootlegs apparel and posters, and possibly, the astronomical ticket prices too.

Along with others in Las Vegas, BrownSugar5 (Sue) heard the fan's touching story about going to shows with her dad when she was standing in line near a "young woman in a pretty pink dress" with her boyfriend. When the fan showed her the black and white shots of her father's gravestone and the engraved lines from "You Can't Always Get What You Want", Sue "started crying for her," in line, and then had "tears streaming down" during the song at the show. Another fan in line from St. Louis was "so nervous he was having reflux", says Sue. She told him to "keep breathing". It was his first time seeing the band. At the end of the show he came up to her, excited to tell her what had happened. He had caught Mick Taylor's guitar pick. "He was elated...great virgin luck," observes Sue.

On the down side, she didn't appreciate having to line up for so long, only to "be treated in such a discourteous manner after paying so much." She is referring to that near mess-up in the order of patrons in the lines, and waiting in at least three different places for long periods after entering the first set of doors into the arena. Each area was less pleasant than the one preceding it, with brusquer staff, as we moved from lines in the carpeted public domain of the MGM Grand Hotel into a large gymnasium, then snaking down the stairs where the line inexplicably doubled outside of two sets of doors. That's where the couple jumped the line and continued to push ahead of others, irritating many. We finally poured into a basement storage area, before ultimately entering the pit at the MGM Grand Theater. Some of the staff seemed bored and hostile, as if we were all long-term inmates lining up for our daily turn in the recreation yard at a maximum-security facility. If most of us didn't have a good idea of the treat awaiting us, we may well have staged an escape. We kept thinking, just wait, everything will work out, and then it did.

On the plus side, after all the waiting, the time in the pit before members of the large drum corps in their gorilla suits marched out was relatively minimal. Jane and I had plenty of time to leave our spots for refreshments and a last bathroom break before the crowd packed into the front. I had a talk with an older usher outside of the pit who painted an unsavory, unappealing picture of his impressions of the women he had seen hanging around the stages waiting for the performers over the years. I couldn't tell if he was disgusted or jealous, or maybe a little of both.

Lottery Winners in the Pit: Hitting the Jackpot with Mystery Tickets

The availability of the 85-dollar seats or the "mystery tickets" or "lottery tickets" started in 2013 in the U.S., perhaps as a method of selling more tickets sooner. One fan called them the "mystery date tickets," because you could only buy the 85s two at a time. For the "14 on Fire tour", they were known as "lucky dips." If you were going alone, you would have to find a partner, someone who would buy a ticket, meet you to wait in line with you to see where your seats were, and then sit next to you during the show. When the mystery tix were announced, they came with the pronouncement that the seat locations would be randomly distributed throughout the venue, location revealed upon pick-up. That seemed true at first, whereas later on, most if not all of the seat locations were in the upper deck. Nonetheless, depending on the venue, a small percentage of fans paying the lowest price hit the mega jackpot, winning the lottery when they learned that their mystery tickets entitled them to join the fans who paid top dollar for the pit.

For many, buying the seats was a no-brainer, since these were the cheapest tickets of all for the concerts. Most people found a friend to go in on the required pair, but some fans advertised their extras or sought out a spare ticket online. A few pooled their two pairs together, stating beforehand that if one or the other fan drew pits with one pair, the hard core fans from the boards would get them, leaving their friends with the other seats.

Some fans tried to psych out the process of attaining the pits, finding out that random envelopes contained the tickets, usually in a separate pile, that would provide them with the coveted wristbands with entry into the pit. At some venues, names for pre-selected pit seats were on a special list, while at others, place in line seemed to determine when someone lucked out and was handed the magic envelope. As the tour went on, fans reported their experiences online, helping people to figure out strategies.

At first the handing out of pit seats seemed completely random, though later some people found that correctly timing their entrance or choosing a particular line, staff member, or window could work. Much variation occurred at different venues, and even among the dates for the same venue. For certain shows, wandering ushers gave pairs or whole groups of fans seated in the "bleacher" stands much better seats in front sections or even awarded them pit tickets. The United Center in Chicago had the ushers who upgraded select fans on opening night there, and staff that allowed box office exchanges. As word went around on this, many people asked ushers for a change of seats, and were told "no" at the second Chicago show, held on a weekend. At the box office line, fans were turned away if they had the lotto tickets. Rumors flew online and offline at shows, some true only for the moment, while individual fans poured through the information coming out daily in each online fan group.

GAFF and his friend left the Shidoobee pre-party a little early to go to the May 18th show in Anaheim, California, making their way over to the small line of people at the 85-dollar ticket line. When they came up to the window, the people in front asked if the process of pulling pit tickets was random. GAFF, an extroverted guy with a thick head of iron gray hair answered, "Yeah, it's random. You either pull pit or you end up in the rafters." When he handed over his ID, the woman checking it turned away to ask a question of one of the other ticket people, and GAFF is thinking he can't believe it, "It's finally going to happen." Then when she tells him to see "the lady in the denim shirt", he's thinking, "Now I KNOW it's gonna happen."

> *She opens the envelope and gives me a BIG smile. I just about shit myself. I could not believe it. It was a totally surreal moment. We got our wristbands and went in and people are high-fiving us right and left.*

They staked out their position at the barrier, on the rail on Keith's side. Later GAFF ran into the usher who had given him a major upgrade for the previous show. Calling him by name, he asked if the usher could help out some of his Shidoobee friends who were up in the rafters. The usher said no, because he was busy managing the floor.

167

Darth Bowie aka Michael DeStafano wrote in detail on Shidoobee about how he found out his 85-dollar lottery tickets turned into pit seats. At the Honda Center in Anaheim, Darth and his brother walked along the north side looking for the $85.00 ticket line. The show would be his brother's first whereas Darth had seen his first show with his father at age 11 during *Steel Wheels* at the LA Coliseum. Now he was 35, nine years older than his brother, and had gone to shows three times since the show in his childhood.

They passed the merchandise stand "with the bands 50th anniversary logo resting on each side" of it. Hearing familiar chord progressions through a glass door that had just swung open, he made "listen-to-that" eyes at his brother. Through the glass he saw a young women unfold a small table inside the venue. He passed fans with tight fists on the handles of black Stones shopping bags.

> *I heard a voice sounding almost as youthful as it did when the song was recorded. The band was rehearsing "Wild Horses," Mick following the ragged twang of Keith's Fender Telecaster. I wanted to stay and listen, but I had an inescapable urge to collect our tickets.*

Darth asked directions to the correct line, and found a long table in the parking lot with a man with gray hair and thin wire-framed eyeglasses behind it. In front of the man were two piles of tickets, "one tall, one short". The man stared at Darth's Sticky Fingers t-shirt as they approached. Standing to the man's right, a woman about the same age as him cradled a clipboard with her right arm. The man announced his name, "Michael DeStefano," and the woman replied, "Found him." She had about a dozen silver wristbands sticking out the neck of her low-cut shirt. As she placed a wristband on his wrist, he thanked her profusely. She responded that it had nothing to do with her, it was just luck, because "it's all random." As he and his brother walked away, Darth thanked her again, and she wished them a great time at the show.

Thinking about how his brother's first show would be from the pit, Darth "was elated, yet jealous."

Conversing with people in line, Darth and his brother met some of the most enthusiastic fans Darth had ever encountered at a shows. Listening to some of his favorite Stones tracks out of the hidden speakers at the entrance, he met "sincere and knowledgeable" fans, some who had paid nearly three thousand dollars for their tickets, and some who had traveled hundreds of miles. He met the German couple that had seen every show of the tour from the pit. He met Justin who was briefly featured in the video that played immediately before the show. He even met a professor from his former college, who said that a colleague of hers had been a back up singer for Ike and Tina Turner and had helped inspire the song "Brown Sugar." A collector of bootlegs impressed him with his familiarity with every one of the live shows and who considered *50 and Counting* their best since 1973. The brothers ended up at the rail, with "Keith's antique Fender amp" right in front of him.

Wembley joked at first that he had "planned every step...his ultimate stealth approach to ensure I got those pit tix. :-)" Then he said he thought getting the tix was completely the luck of the draw, with each mystery ticket holder having about a one in twenty chance of winning pits. He had seen a seating chart on Shidoobee tracking the tickets for shows before this, and virtually all of the non-pits in Anaheim were "Section 400s, upper nosebleeds," exactly what they got for their previous shows. Wembley noted that the current "ticket distribution goes against what was posted on the Stones website originally" before the mystery tickets were sold. The notice said mystery tickets were assigned randomly to locations "throughout" the venue, including the pit. Wembly said that was true opening night at Staples in LA, but nowhere else. The two alternatives were in fact either "a handful of upgrades " or "Ticket Siberia", as he called the upper-level placements.

Hearing that 7 p.m. seemed a good time to arrive for previous pit winners, Wembley went up to the ticket window about that time. Diane had to work during the week, so he took a friend from LA to this Wednesday evening show. At the shows up to now, they would check off his name from his ID, and they would hand him a ticket. This time the person picks up the envelope, holds it up and

signals another lady off to the side, then tells me to step around to the side, The envelope is passed to second lady without me touching it. At this point, since I've heard about previous transactions, I pretty much know these are pit upgrades and that is confirmed when the envelope is opened.

The friend knew there was a small chance of pits, but hadn't expected it, and "was delighted." Wembley soon decided, "after his thought processes cleared a bit" from the excitement, that he might need earplugs if he was standing so close to the music. They stopped at the first aid office where he nabbed two sets, went to concessions to buy beverages, and headed downstairs to enter the pit. Once there, he knew that "the pit is THE place to be." Even though you have to stand, he found a space leaning against the left edge of the fence or wall of the tongue rim facing the stage on Ronnie's side, and was "quite comfortable there the whole night."

Having been in the pit before, I found a woman named Susan online who had an extra mystery ticket and went for it in Philadelphia, night one. I also had another ticket in the stands, my side bet, a very good seat that I would sell to another fan at a cheap price when he came in on our deal, if by any chance we hit pits, a long shot. Now I had a plan to meet up with two strangers who had posted on Shidoobee. Walking in the rain, I looked for a pre-party of Shidoobee in the vast parking lot of the Wells Fargo Center but couldn't find it. Instead I ran into some really, really nice people tailgating in a sheltered area who took pity on me, cooking me a hamburger and giving me a beer. Coming in for the show from northern PA, super-friendly Thomas Krisa, his wife, friends and I ate, drank, and laughed together, exchanging Stones stories as we sat in folding chairs on their makeshift patio. I then hightailed it over to XFINITY in the stadium area to join the crowd watching the excellent tribute band The Glimmer Twins. Walking right up to the front to have a close look at the band, the one guy in on the ticket deal with us found me there, spotting me soon after I arrived in my black Stones cowboy hat. Fans who recognized me were very friendly, including Bernie Bollendorf as Keith Richards, who gave me a shout-out from his mic onstage. After a while we had to leave to join the 85-dollar ticket line.

Connecting by cell phone, Susan was going to meet us in line. We came to the front and inside before she arrived, so I told my ticket buddy to wait while I went outside again, even though we were told not to leave once we had entered the building. I slipped out anyway, telling the questioning security guy that I was looking for my "ticket partner." I saw Susan then, standing about a dozen people back, waved, and she joined me inside. I just had a funny sensation since everything had a special feeling that night, that we might hit it big. No expectations, I kept saying to myself. Even when the ticket lady asked who was with Susan and I said, "Me," I'm thinking I see wristbands but I still can't believe it. Sure enough! We were in. The nice guy with us happily bought my other ticket, a very good seat for only 85 dollars, the deal we had. As we were walking away, I heard a Shidoobee friend yelling "Andee, are you in the pit?" and I said "Yeah, " hardly believing it. A few days later, an usher gave him and some of his buddies pit tickets for Philly 2, an even better show than mine, the fans agreed.

Our show in Philly 1 was plenty good. Too late to snag a front view, I thought leaning against the side or back barrier would work best. Susan and I headed for the back rim, which happened to have a small ledge in front of it, increasing my short height by a few inches. From our perch on the center back rim slightly toward Ronnie's side, we could see the stage, and had very close views of band members mainly Mick, and also

Keith and Ronnie coming around the tongue. By this time, the third last show on the American leg of the tour, Mick was prancing around the rim so frequently and so fast that I even missed a turn or two of his as he came by, only catching him on his trip back to the stage. The down side of that location came later in the show when more fans crowded into the back of the pit, which was quite roomy for the first half. The drunkenness quotient of the crowd had increased, as one tall guy demonstrated dance steps for his buddies, moving back and forth, blocking the view. A woman teetered in and out of the pit, too wasted to keep her balance, depending on the crowd to hold her up.

Johnny Caito couldn't believe how hard it could be to get rid of an 85-dollar ticket, even if the show was not on a weekend. Finally the morning of his show, a person from the Shidoobee board told him he needed Johnny's extra for his second friend. They decided each of them would take whichever were the best seats of the two pairs they had purchased, and they would give the friends the other pair.

When they approached the ticket counter, Johnny "kindly begged for pit tickets." No wristband appeared. Johnny then said "Oh that's not good news. No wristbands, no pit tickets."

> *But then, just to the side of me, my new Stones buddy quietly said, "We're in the pit. We got pit tickets." The employee who was handing out the wristband asked who else was with him, and I became the lucky winner of the golden ticket! "Thank ya Jesus, than you, Lord."*

If not for the last minute arrangement, Johnny found that his own tickets were in those upper deck rafters. As the workers placed the wristbands onto them, it clicked with Johnny that he was in the pit. His reaction? "Exhilaration. Thrilled. Excitement."

As they made their way down the aisle and into the tongue pit, everything became "very surreal" says Johnny. He'd been close but "this time it felt like we really hit the jackpot." Even once the show started, his brain could hardly compute that he'd made it into the pit.

Among others who had pit tickets purchased for full price at other shows before testing their luck on the 85s, IGTBA waited in the will call line. He soon found himself in another line at the side after a "lady lifted up the envelope cover, looked at my tickets...and kept my ID with the ticket envelope." He saw a helper call the name of one of the two people in front of him and pull out their wristbands, and thought "This might be great--and it was!!!" IGTBA noticed that quite a few people in Oakland got pit seats with their 85s, and then again, there were well over 1,000 people who went through the 85 line, "maybe over 2K."

Danny describes his luck during "one if the craziest nights of his life." He waited in line for over an hour, when he was finally handed a white envelope of tickets that said "GA PIT!!!" he writes. The tickets were numbered out of a total of 50, "meaning only 25 pairs of GA PIT tickets were given out to the people who purchased the 85-dollar tickets" out of the 1000 sold, he explains. He found the tongue pit almost empty when he went in, ending up in the second row, dead center in front of Mick.

Working with the box office in Chicago, Scott and his friend picked up their 85s at 6:30 p.m. and were handed seats located behind the stage, at the "very, very top of the arena." He went to the indoor box office and within 60 seconds "had two seats in the pit." He ended up in the second row right in front of Keith. Scott compliments the venue: "Great work, UC box office."

Most others were not so fortunate. After missing pits by one spot in line, with the wristbands going to the couple behind us, 3DTeafoe (Daniel) and I tried to exchange our upper level tix too, at the United Center on the same night as Scott, for Chicago 2, May 31st. We had no luck, with either the wandering ushers or with the box office. We did do a "self-upgrade," and would have aimed for a closer view on the lower stands or even the floor, but I was uneasy doing that, especially before the show had started. Wembley calls the self-upgrading or relocating "negotiating" for a better seat. We had already occupied two seats in a lower section soon claimed by their real owners, us apologizing before vacating to a nearby spot. Rather than strike out alone to explore more desirable seats, Daniel kindly stayed with me, the out-of-towner. I had never seen a show from the center back of the auditorium, a straight shot to the stage, in the first section above the floor. They played "Can't You Hear Me Knocking" that night, one of my favorites, with superb sound in the UC.

Pointing out different strategies, Wembley ended up buying better-priced seats in the lower level, along with the 85s. Mentioning this on the Shidoobee board, he worked out a deal to sell and exchange tickets inside the venue. Later on he learned about the kind of self-upgrading that included getting a better ticket from a box office person or usher, something he had not heard of until this tour, or "just finding empty seats downstairs" and squeezing in. In the future, Wembley says he would probably pass on the 85s, even with a chance at pits if he was buying for the two of them. Diane refuses to sit in the rafters anymore, where they "wound up for three shows" and she is more uncomfortable than me with trying to self-upgrade by changing seats, rejecting that tactic entirely. But then again, because of how inexpensive the tickets are, he still might try it again if he was going by himself.

On successful relocations, I know of two people who walked into the pit, past security, without legitimate tickets or wristbands. At Newark 2, sitting in the stands on the side, I saw a fan follow a band member's daughter down the stairs of a side section with her permission, straight into the pit toward the end of the show. The two had become acquainted at other venues in New York City. They had chatted on a number of occasions so she knew him and apparently offered to help him into the desirable area.

In another father/daughter story, I also know a father who I met in line in Newark 1 with his daughter who became a fan through her dad's love of the band. Later I noticed her standing behind me, in the second row of the pit, and asked her where her father was. "Oh, he's coming," she said, and a while later, she left her position, soon returning with him. His daughter didn't have a celebrity connection like the other daughter. What she did was undo her own wristband, taking it off and giving it to her dad who taped it back together in the restroom, and proceeded to wear it in. She apparently walked back in without displaying her wrist, recognized by the usher. Months later in Las Vegas, the same father greeted me me as he passed by the line for the pit. He tried but did not manage to enter the pit later on because he couldn't convince a friend who brought his son there to smuggle the wristband out. He couldn't match the wristband's writing to concoct a fake one. Since none of his 85s panned out with good seats, this father still self-upgraded during the five shows where he didn't make it into the pit.

Reactions of the Fans to the Shows from the Pit

Within the pit, responses were overwhelmingly positive. Beast had never had such a fantastic, close-up experience, including her club shows. Ellen called the pit experience "one of the highlights" of her life, allowing that this statement "might sound shallow to the uninitiated." Wembley prefers club gigs for their smaller stages and audiences. Placement within the crowd at each venue can make a difference in someone's reaction, along with the quality of interaction with people before, during and after the shows. Those who converted from 85 seats to pit tickets express more excitement just before going in than those expecting a great experience from the start, but otherwise the two groups were equally impressed with the shows.

The front of the pit allows people to see all the small interactions among the band members, from short joking comments and movements that you see even if you can't hear, to small gestures from one band member to another, to stagehands picking up the clothes as Mick discards them. The expressions on each musician's face are on view, telegraphing how they feel playing or singing at every moment, and their responses to interactions with the crowd and individuals within it. You can see Mick signal the other musicians every time the end of the song is imminent. My front row pit in Las Vegas showed me every little interaction between Mick Jagger and guest performer Katy Perry. At one point, he flicked the back of her hair up with his hand and she reacted with a slight smile and an eye blink. He seemed to know just how far he could go in his teasing, given on the one hand, her huge stage presence, and demonstrated poise, with on the other hand, her very young age and the fact they had first met at a rehearsal only hours before. When Keith shows his appreciation for the crowd reaction on his featured spot, you can not only hear the repeated shouts of "Keef!" but you can also feel all the love from the audience directed to him, and then catch and feel the sincerity of the warmth that Keith shoots back. HIs smile and gestures complement his words of gratitude, straight from the heart.

The closest I ever "sat" or stood before the pit was in seats in the second row on the side and fifth row on the floor, although I once watched part of a show from the first row next to the B stage. For a complete show, the pit was closer, so close that the front row for a short person meant not seeing Charlie at all, and rarely seeing some of the others. The back of the pit on the barrier, front row on the lower lip when we turned to the back, gave me a really close view of whoever walked around it, mainly Mick. What a treat!

With Susan, my new 85-dollar buddy, I ended up on the official tape of this show a few times, once spotlighted for ten seconds during the taping of "Emotional Rescue" in Philly 1. As Mick danced in front of us, I grinned and waved my arms in time with him, and Susan snapped photos. That was an unanticipated souvenir of the *50 and Counting* tour, something to show my brother, and to know our attendance was a preserved part of Stones history. I'll take the pit any time, when I can have the front rail, or if not there, the side at the wall near the front, or what I had in Philly, at the back barrier with a raised area. Otherwise I won't have a place to lean for hours, and I doubt if I'd be able to see from the middle, with my height of 5' 2".

Most in the people in the pit are focused on the show, definitely in the front, and even in the back, with the few exceptions of people who are too drunk to care much, like two people I saw in Chicago. At the very front, a dedicated fan can avoid most interruptions of the show, standing with other equally transfixed fans. Before the 85s came into the mix after the start of the tour, pits were much less full, allowing freer movement of fans who desired different vantage points during the show.

The tremendous rush right before the band comes on is always a memorable moment for me, and in the pit at the front rail, it takes a while to adjust to the band playing and singing so near. Even before that, entering the pit area of the audience in the dark, and seeing the stage so close is thrilling. Watching them as they take their places onstage is almost like a hallucination except it's really happening. At my show from the back of the pit in Philly, an usher in his early twenties with his eyes fixed on the stage told us early on that this show was by far the best concert he had ever seen, and I told him that's why we were here.

When Wembley walked in after his 85s became pits he saw a lot of space around the outer tongue section. Like me, he purposely picked out a place to lean. He found the sound excellent though he thought the earlier show in Las Vegas was better. In his analytic fashion, he summed up how the recent shows flowed, assuming no major glitches: "They run like a well-oiled machine." He did appreciate the playing of "Champagne and Reefer" with John Mayer, "definitely a bonus!"

People in the pit raved about seeing the expressions on band members' faces. Brownsugar5 loved blowing kisses to everybody and "having them blow them back and wink at me." She celebrated her birthday from the front rail. Another fan said his mind was so blown to see all the guys so close that he was still in shock from the experience following the concert. Still a Fool proclaimed how amazing it is to be so close, adding, "It's really hard to get bored when you're that close watching the Stones' every facial expression," even on the songs he's heard live over forty times.

Johnny Caito told me how he usually listens to "every little detail in the music," but from the pit

I watched facial expressions, chord progressions, drum fills, and details. I watched as Keith's eyes would follow Mick, looking for certain cues, and watched the joy on the faces of thousands of fans.

Grateful to hear the "gems" of "Champagne and Reefer" like Wembley, and also "Rocks Off" that surprised him with its opening riff, what struck Johnny even more was his impression of why the band keeps playing:

Seeing them this close, you get a true feel of how much they love thestage. Yes, the money is big. The pay-out is huge. But when you can see the whites of their eyeballs, you can see passion; you can see a band that loves what they do.

Johnny Caito also praises Mick, saying how seeing him close makes him seem ever better than before. He speaks of the "electric" energy, showmanship and "incredibly strong" voice throughout of the greatest front man rock and roll has ever seen.

Feeling as if Mick was singing directly to her, Joanne screamed between songs, "Mick, we love you! You are so hot!" The woman behind her kept telling her to keep it up, since Mick could hear her. Joanne said her reaction was hard to characterize. "It was unexplainable. It felt like a dream." Joanne felt lucky to see Mick Taylor playing along on "Sway." She would like to repeat her pit experience at another show, though perhaps from farther back because she could see Keith only a few times, and Charlie not at all from front row center.

Spotting Bernard's wife and daughter in the pit, GAFF "hung out, sipped a cocktail, and soaked it all in." He saw Chuck just behind the backstage area and went to ask for a photo with him. "Nice guy, Chuck is," says GAFF. He calls "Bitch" with Dave Grohl, a "barnburner," the perfect combination of a surprise guest and song. "That boy fucking shreds," observes GAFF of Grohl. He teared up when Keith joined by Ronnie did "You Got the Silver." GAFF describes the whole experience of the show as "beautiful and fulfilling and sublime and magical and spiritual and uplifting and absolutely fucking amazing," nearly beyond belief.

Going to five shows, all in the pit, benstones became the recipient of repeated interactions from the band. He reflects back on the concerts:

> *First of all, the stage is fabulous. Second of all, I had the guitar picks of Keith AND Ronnie. It is priceless for me...Keith saw me and made winks to me many times. Again, it is priceless!!! Lisa made a heart with her hands to me! She sent me kisses too!*

Benjamin acknowledges, like Joanne, that he could have a better view from the third or 4th row, but that the front row is "something special and unique."

Known as Darth Bowie on Shidoobee, Michael DeStefano wrote extensively about his reaction to his show experiences, from the opening film to the closing chords of "Satisfaction". He notes the difference in hearing the sound of the band from newer recordings of live shows to being right there in the pit, in front of the band, saying

> *I realized that no live recording from the last forty years had faithfully reproduced the sound I was hearing from the stage.*

179

What I was hearing was the raw wallop captured on live recordings such as Get Yer Ya-Ya's Out *(1969) and* The Brussel's Affair *(1973).*

Like Johnny, Darth became aware of the "telepathic" nature of communication as he watches the eyes of Mick, Keith and Charlie:

Keith is the band-leader. Charlie follows Keith, and Mick relies on Charlie to keep a song chugging along at its proper speed. Before entering a chorus or bridge, or conclusion of a song, Mick glances at Charlie who then reconnects with Keith.

He says that Ronnie taps into the whole by eyeing all three. The process repeats itself as each song unfolds within the set.

Thrilled that Keith threw a pick to him, Darth had a struggle to retrieve it from among the cables between the stage and the barrier to the pit. Not wanting to trouble the cameraman, he asked a security guard to pick it up for him, but he refused. When the house lights came on after the show, he saw the cameraman breaking down his equipment and told him, "Keith threw me his pick but it landed in your cords...Can I please have it?" When the cameraman looked where Darth was pointing and reached for the pick, Darth thought at first he would keep it for himself, but he "placed it into my hand." It was a white pick with the tongue and Mick Taylor's name on the other side. As he slid it into a deep sleeve inside his wallet, he walked out of the pit with his brother, thinking the pick was "one of the most priceless mementos he could ever have."

Overall Thoughts on the Pit

Considering that most fans love to see the band live more than hearing them on recordings, this opportunity of the pit represents the pinnacle of fandom to many. Even those who had seen them in the front rows of shows before felt closer to the band than that, securing front rows in the pit. The chance to see the whole band interact or to focus on your favorite admired from afar, sometimes for decades, proved worthwhile.

While some lucked out with their cheaper tickets, though not as many as ticket-buyers were led to believe by promoters, even those who paid full price did not regret their decision. Fans have protested rising ticket costs over the years, some dropping out of the game entirely, and the rest grudgingly accepting the jump in prices. This time the difference between a pit ticket and an expensive seat in the "front" rows behind the pit, though not trivial, seemed well worth the cost to those who had observed audiences on videotapes.

One man who was in a few pit locations compared them to conclude that the O2 was his favorite because the uncertainty of seeing them again and then "all of a sudden, they're back!" He enjoyed the second Chicago show for the quality of the playing, "Off the charts."

"Role-Embracement" of Fans

As a counterpoint to his idea of "role distance" when a person would visibly demonstrate his separation from a role, the sociologist Erving Goffman (1961) explained the opposite case of "role embracement." He used this term to describe when an individual fits the expected behaviors and attitudes of a social role so well role that the person and the role would merge and become one. To achieve this state, a role has to be easy enough to perform competently, and yet, challenging enough to hold the person's interest. If this is true, the person embraces the role or hugs it, pulls it close. Otherwise, someone would physically show discomfort with a role, or "role distance." In such a case, for example, a family member called upon to make a spontaneous toast at a reunion might mutter to the crowd beforehand that he had never done this before or how he wasn't very good at these things. He is telling those gathered, please don't confuse me with this role of a toastmaster, because I am better than that.

To me, a hardcore Stones devotee, epitomized by at least some of the pit patrons, shows role embracement, a merging with the role of "Stones fan." The fan is willing to pay a very high cost, not only monetary, but in the time deciding to procure the tickets, waiting in line for hours before gaining entrance, and keeping the place secured before and during the show, not to mention standing up for very long periods. At least among other fans, pit fans, fans who attend club shows, and other hard core fans are proud of the role of The Rolling Stones fan, often wearing apparel announcing their allegiance and adopting Stones-related usernames and avatars online, showing the "attachment" component of role embracement (Goffman, 1961). They research and share information on the Stones, their lives, and their music, noting details about each bootleg and official recording as it is released, participating in "demonstration," role embracement's second manifestation. The last element of role embracement is "engagement," certainly revealed by the physical actions of going to concerts and in this case assuring themselves a sure pit spot or a possibility of one.

This role embracement concept can be usefully applied to fans of other bands, TV series or individual celebrities to shed light on which elements they have in common, and which are different. The portrait of fans here can help fill in what people in the first decades of the 20th century do in their pursuit of "serious leisure" (Stebbins, 1992), in their dedication to activities outside of paid work.

PHOTOS OF FANS WITH BAND MEMBERS

(by row, from top left, fan listed first)

I. FANS WITH CORE BAND AND BACK UP MUSICIANS
Set A
- Glenn and Mick
- nursejane and Ronnie
- Gimme Lil Drink and Ronnie
- Cindy Jagger and Keith
- Jimmy B and Charlie
- Exile Brian, Keith and Bobby Keys

Set B
- Cindy Jagger and Mick
- Gazza and Charlie
- Bill German and Bill Wyman
- GAFF and Chuck Leavell
- Stonesdoug and Bernard Fowler
- Blue Lena, Bernard Fowler and Blondie Chaplin

Set C
- BitchKeepsBitchin and Mick Taylor
- stonesmarie and Bobby Keys
- Gerardo and Mick Taylor
- Gazza and Darryl Jones
- Theo and Lisa Fischer
- Blue Lena and Tim Ries

III. FANS AT MEET AND GREETS AND OTHER OCCASIONS
   Set D
- Vilhelm and The Stones
- Moongoddess and The Stones
- Little Queenie, Ronnie and Keith
- colditalianpizza and Keith

   Set E
- Nandita, Mick and Charlie
- Gail and Keith
- Nandita and Charlie

IV. FANS IN THE AUDIENCE AT SHOWS
   Set F
- Beast, Kahoosier, Mick and Keith
- Calista's hand
- Flairville and Mick

Set A

Andrea Baker

Set B

Set D

Set E

Set F

CHAPTER SEVEN:

"I JUST WANT TO SEE HIS FACE: UP CLOSE AND PERSONAL ENCOUNTERS WITH THE STONES"

"Then Keith walked up to me and I said 'Gold rings on ya,' and he said 'Gold rings on ya too.'" (RainingBlimps)

The greatest fan dream is often to meet a real live Rolling Stone face-to-face. There are formal "Meet and Greets" where a fan has about ten seconds to shake a hand or mumble a few words. There are the almost by-chance or serendipitous meetings in a Stones hotel or outside of a venue. Of course fans usually must position themselves in an advantageous spot for many hours or be able to afford to stay at the posh hotel of the band to create such a "happy accident." Once in a great while, a fan who performs services for either a band member or the whole band is able to penetrate through the outer layers of the Stones organization into the inner circle. The most noteworthy example of this case is Bill German who turned from a teen-aged chronicler into an acknowledged member of the Stones group, writing about them in the hard copy fanzine *Beggar's Banquet*. At its peak, Bill mailed his independently produced newsletter to between 3,000 and 4,000 subscribers. He describes in depth his journey from high school devotee to editor of the official Stones newsletter, then reaching 20,000 fans, to his leaving the band's orbit in his 2009 book *Under Their Thumb*.

Contact with Band Members at a Special Event, Through Work, and Running a Website

At times, a fan has a chance to meet a band member on a special occasion, outside of events taking place before or after a show. When CandyFromStrangers (CandyFS) won a radio contest for free tickets and transportation to the *Shine A Light* film premiere and press conference, she took advantage of the opportunity to go just a little further. Winning was an iffy deal since she was the eighth person on the station's list to call. You had to be ready to leave for New York City in two days during the week, and possess an up-to-date passport. The seven people who turned the opportunity down included one guy with a drug conviction and others who had to work. Aside from seeing the premiere, CandyFS wanted a one-to-one contact with a certain Rolling Stone, although she wasn't sure how that could happen. Here's what went on, as it took place.

She was at the press conference listening to the comments of the band and the film director, exciting enough, seated eleven rows back on the aisle, among the others in the thirteen rows of audience chairs set up for the occasion. She struck up a conversation with the PR guy from Paramount, hoping for her chance to connect with a band member, but that didn't happen. She hopped on a bus taking the twenty fans over to the movie theater. No one had expected the band to appear onstage at the second spot, but, by this time, CandyFS was clued in.

She found herself in the sparsely populated upstairs lobby of the uptown IMAX Theater showing the U.S. premiere of the documentary, and could scarcely believe her eyes when a line of four individuals appeared, quickly moving into a corridor. They were all thin as rails and about the same height, 5' 8", estimates CandyFS, herself on the tall side. The PR movie guy from Paramount has alerted her that this is more or less a private space but that he will let her stay. She does have a badge but they both know it is an audience badge rather than an insider pass, even if it does say "VIP." There is a whole hierarchy of badges, from the Meet and Greet to backstage pass to all-access pass when the shows are going on. Even the badges from the fan club Shidoobee may look official to the uninformed. I had one in Las Vegas before the show, and people would ask directions and other questions, thinking I was with the tour. That behavior was most common when I stayed at the MGM Grand venue where the band played, walking the halls without my purse. A laminated badge hanging down from a lanyard looks like a pass to sought-after realms of the connected. In CandyFS's case, the Paramount movie badge was visually identical to the Paramount badges, "the same" as her *Shine a Light* guest fan badge.

CandyFS thought she saw Keith's grey fedora peaking out from a small curtain, and sure enough, all four of the Stones have come out from the backstage area, walking into the dark hall going into the theater. She followed them in there, aware of the "massive" security guys, trying not to stare at the boys. Charlie and Ronnie were clowning around, and Mick, ever hyperactive was "bouncing up and down." She fell into the line right beside Keith.

> *...after they started moving into the theatre I walked beside Keith and said "Hello." Big smile, hug around the shoulder and handshake. "Hello, Luv!" He was pulled a few feet forward by one of the others and then we were all waiting in the hall/ tunnel for the introductions to start. It was a lousy place to ask anything - the security people could have tossed me. I waited until after the introductions when they were leaving.*

CandyFS would try to pick the best moment to deliver a present to Keith. Some fans such as BL had given him scarves over the years decorated with the skull symbol, and he has appeared at curtain calls with those around his neck. Collaborating with another fan on the design, this gift CandyFS waited to hand-deliver was born out of a meeting in London in the summer of 2007 during the last concerts on the ABB tour. An Australian fan who resembled Keith and indeed, had met him, Rockman had the idea for an inscription on a t-shirt CandyFS wanted to create for Keith.

So... there I am standing in the tunnel of the theatre, t-shirt in hand, waiting for Keith to come out. He's right in front of me, against the wall, and I say "Keith, you may have heard of a certain 'Rockman' in Australia. Thought this would give you a laugh..." He takes it and leaves. Our Paramount guy says that later as they were leaving the area, the woman with Keith still had it in her hand.

Encased in a zip-lock bag, the t-shirt had a graphic on its front. The image was a cropped version of a well-known black and white headshot of Keith leaning slightly back against a wall, the omnipresent cigarette dangling from his mouth. He wears a leopard print shirt, with a narrow Japanese silk scarf draped over it. Tied on his neck is a dark, over-sized bowtie with white polka dots. Rockman took the image for his avatar at IORR, following each of his posts there. The portrait was displayed in Terry Southern's 1978 book *The Rolling Stones on Tour,* with photographs by Christopher Sykes and Annie Leibovitz. Thirty years later, Sebastian Kruger used it to create his artwork, in full color, naming it "The Fugitive." On the front of the bagged-up t-shirt's white background, over Keith's face above the picture, the black lettering reads "WHO THE FUCK IS..." and then "ROCKMAN" below it, in larger block letters.

When Candy FS handed the gift to Keith, what a nice moment for fans, for the guy whose name is on the shirt and for CandyFS who's giving the gift directly to Keith, and really, for all of us who can chuckle later at the anecdote, living vicariously through them. Of course, the shirt is a put-on of the original photo of Keith wearing a "Who the Fuck is Mick Jagger?" shirt. Keith had it on under a hooded jacket immortalized in Sykes and Leibovitz' work during the *Tour of the Americas.* His face framed by the hood in the shot, his eyes half closed, he is smoking something that looks like a thickly rolled joint, both hands on his hips. Before the t-shirt, Keith knew the Aussie fan Rockman well enough to dedicate a song to him onstage, the rarest of accolades from The Riffmaster. Keith had said his name, "This one's for Rockman," before launching into "The Worst."

Currently selling Ronnie Wood's artwork, Matt Lee is a UK collector of memorabilia and recordings. Matt and Ronnie first connected over a dozen years ago, and have been in contact ever since. Matt has met Ronnie over a hundred times, and once, they even went Christmas shopping together. Ronnie told Matt he could call him any time, since he has his personal phone number. Matt has not taken advantage of that access, not at all, only texting him twice in the first six months. Matt considers himself just a fan that got a break, someone who found himself a role that is useful to the Stones. He says he is a businessman. He is known to have better prices on Ronnie's artwork than are available elsewhere.

Matt discussed how even if you have an "all access" pass that is better than a Rattlesnake Inn badge, people can still challenge your presence. In his book, Bill German told of how he felt unwelcome after a point even though he had done the Stones newsletter for so many years. Never as much of an insider, but performing his role for Ronnie, Matt experienced something similar. One time in Ireland, people who had the stickers on were admitted to the Rattlesnake Inn but were told to leave right after it. Matt had the laminate pass and decided since his friends were going, he would too. However, when the person running the organic hot dog stand right outside started by Ronnie's then-wife Jo offered him a hot dog and he lingered, a security guard told him he had to go. The man said, "Just because you have laminate doesn't mean you take advantage of it." Matt told him to go take the pass to Ronnie and tell him why you took it. The guy didn't know whom he might piss off by confiscating Matt's pass. That action removed the fun of being there at that moment. "That took the shine off it," says Matt. After noting that incident, Matt described his relationship to the security personnel:

The ones that don't know me treat me with respect because I've got a laminate. As soon as they know you're a fan who got lucky...they treat you like shit.... if you treat me like a human being, just tell me and I'll move.

Matt doesn't post much but fans at both Shidoobee and IORR often refer to him when anyone wants to buy Rolling Stones art, particularly that of Ronnie Wood. As noted, he offers good prices to serious fans of the band and has access to older artwork along with new work as soon as Ronnie produces it.

Another person who connects with individual band members as part of his full-time occupation, is DurtySox or Glenn Schneider. He is a freelance photographer and videographer formerly with an independent firm that does jobs for television networks and movie production companies. His co-workers knew what a big fan he is, so they always hoped he nabbed the shoots with the Stones when they came up. When the band is on tour in the States, this could happen more regularly. Since Glenn lives in New York City, a major global center for media including music, advertising, and television, he is positioned well to document publicity gigs for celebrities. Because his clients know he is a fan since his grade school days, they can sometimes line him up for Stones appearances.

He has a shot taken with Mick that shows him "bug-eyed," but he doesn't care. How many of us have that chance to have our picture taken with Mick Jagger? He turned one version of it into a blue-washed photo. He worked with Mick during his 2004 interviews on the remake of the Alfie film with Jude Law replacing Michael Caine and music composed by Mick Jagger, Dave Stewart and John Powell.

Like CandyFS, Glenn was at the shoot for the press conference and premiere of *Shine a Light*. Once he was notified of scheduled shoots for the documentary, he chose to work with Keith, precisely since he had already had the spot with Mick. At the press conference, he found an unoccupied stool behind a mass of reporters, granting him access to good shots of the band. Before the movie premiere at the theater a few blocks away, he directed Lisa Fisher and Albert Maysles to the front of the red carpet from where they had wandered behind the scenes. This time, he and Keith bantered together for a while, fan-musician to musician-celebrity. Glenn plays guitar in a local band. For souvenirs of the shoots, with the help of the crew, Glenn took some of the backdrops home, large cardboard graphics, very heavy to carry, along with Keith's ashtray and cigarettes. He called the two-day shoot, "the best two days of his working life," only comparable to the day with Mick.

So far in his shows between 1981 and 2006 and his various video gigs, Glenn has met most of the Stones and some of the back-up personnel. He summarizes his good fortune in his online profile: "I Shook hands with MICK, KEITH & RONNIE, Daryl, Bernard, Blondie, Alexandra Richards. I Just need Charlie!"

Demonstrating her devotion to Keith Richards through "the Keith shrine" she maintains online, Blue Lena or BL, or Tamara, has met the man known as "the human riff" a number of times. The main fan site has moved from a website to an interactive Facebook page called "The Keith Shrine with Blue Lena" with over 2300 members. She still keeps the website started in 1996 on tripod.com too, now primarily a personal journal of her adventures at shows and gatherings, and she has a couple of early pages at angelfire.com. BL's history with Keith and the band in person begins with her initial show in Philly on the *Voodoo Lounge* tour. For the first time, she saw the band live, and was thrilled to hear "Wild Horses," a song she had hoped they would play.

Andrea Baker

During the next tour, she managed to give Keith a few of her scarves, either by handing them directly to him from the audience, or sending the scarves backstage to Keith through an intermediary. She gave her first scarf to him in Columbus in 1997 after a security guard ripped the film out of her camera, as she looked on, horrified. Another security guard, sympathetic since the ruckus with the camera, let her stand "pressed against the catwalk near her seat. She shook hands with Chuck and Darryl as they came down the catwalk toward the B-Stage. She and her friend had waved the skull scarf throughout the show. When Keith walked right in front of her, she held her arm straight out, with the scarf in hand, and

simultaneously my friends and I all yelled "KEITH!". I was utterly amazed when Keith bent down, took the scarf from my hand, touching my knuckles to his, then stood up, turned and looked me in the eyes and touched his fist to his head and heart in gratitude.

BL "melted on the spot." She was in ecstasy, having waited for that moment since the late seventies, when she became aware of the band, when the music entered her consciousness.

When her third row seats became first row on Keith's side in Philly that same year, she gave him another scarf. He wore it for the final bow, Keith and the scarf captured up on the big screen for all to see at the end of the show. Giving Keith special scarves became an ongoing tradition, continuing through all the tours she was able to attend.

BL met Charlie first in 1996 after his Tentet in Toronto show. In March 1999 in Philly, Blue Lena got her first VIP pass, and an invitation to Marilou's Voodoo CrewDoo crew band party. Not until a little later that spring of 1999 in Columbus, Ohio did she get her first band lounge pass, driving in for the show through the rain after the Cleveland show the night before. She met Charlie for the second time backstage there,

198

bringing his *Long Ago and Far Away* promo CD with her. Modest and shy, not one to seek attention, right before he signed it, Charlie asked, "Where did you get that?"

At the 1999 Philly CrewDoo party for Stones personnel and the back-up band, Mick showed up and BL found herself and her friends about five feet away from him. While the backing band played, they "got to dance for Mick." They didn't dare speak to him. BL and her friends Elizabeth and Joe said "Hi" to Mick as he left his hotel in Philly in 2002, and he said "Hi" back. Since then, BL has seen Mick many times in person and up close, but has not spoken to him, "other than a hello."

After seeing Ronnie in the hotel in1999 in Philly, BL rode the hotel elevator with him in Cleveland that same year. Many encounters with Ronnie since then have included the time during the *Shine a Light* weekend in NYC when she gave him an issue of the *Stones Planet* Fanzine. He kissed her then, and kissed and hugged her goodnight at the end of the movie after-party.

Last but certainly not least of the big four, "Keith, of course, is the main person I wanted to meet, " says Blue Lena. She first saw him up close, in person in Pittsburgh in 1999. Getting into his van, he gave her a wave. In the same city, four years later, she spoke to him when he arrived at his hotel. Then that year, in 2003, she had her first meeting with him. He thanked her for the scarf he took from her during the show the night before, giving her a kiss. Then backstage in 2005, Keith and BL hugged in San Francisco.

Finally in 2006 she had a private meeting with Keith backstage at the MGM Grand, where she posed for photos with him, just the two of them. Once before she had a similar photo op before the show, but security there in Boston made her turn in her camera. At the Las Vegas venue, after waiting for the call to come over, BL decided to try calling instead. She was asked where she was, and soon found herself behind the backstage inner curtain moving up the backstage hallway. By now it was close to show time. She hurried and yet had that "slow motion" feeling. She entered a room marked "Wardrobe," standing in the doorway, not talking to anyone who passed by. Soon she was told to get her camera ready for pictures.

She saw Keith coming around the corner, looking "fantastic and ever the pirate, with a huge smile." Taking the scarf she offered him, Keith immediately draped it around his neck, greeting her with a bear hug, and a "Hello, dahling." When BL thanked Keith for letting her see him, he said, "Thank YOU, you keep on giving, and all I do is accept."

For the first photos in Las Vegas, Keith has on his aviator shades, removing them for the rest of the pictures. He has a skull scarf around his neck, this one an abstract skull print, gifted to him by BL. In the photo, Keith sports Stones colors, his red and black headband patterned from the Japanese flag, along with the red, black, and white scarf. Not yet dressed for the stage, he wears a plum-colored tee with grey-stripes under a crushed green velvet vest. She is in a black and white top embellished with a silver-sequined skull with red crossbones. Both are wearing silver accessories, his skull ring, hair ornament, and watch complementing her rings and pendant.

After the photo, she couldn't stop smiling. Neither could he. Keith was in such a good mood, so friendly, so at ease, just the way she had hoped he would be. She kept thanking him and then burst out with the lyrics from "Far Away Eyes":

"Thank You Jesus, Thank You Lord!" and Keith laughed out loud and said "Don't thank THEM!" obviously not connecting it to the song lyric, to which I replied "Thank you Keith!

She still can't believe it happened, "the best Stones experience ever."

Within the backing band or "Band 2", BL has met everyone except trumpet player Kent Smith. She met singer/guitarist Blondie Chaplin first in 1997, and singer Bernard Fowler soon after. She is acquainted with keyboardist Chuck Leavell, and bassist Darryl Jones, part of the "core band", with Mick, Keith, Ronnie and Charlie.. She has also talked with saxophonist Bobby Keys, singer Lisa Fisher, trombonist, Michael Davis, and Tim Ries on saxophone and keyboards. She has clocked the most hours in Blondie's company, and spent time with Chuck backstage when he was playing with Gov't Mule in Cleveland. When Bobby played in California with Levon Helm, she and her friends hung out there with Bobby. She has promoted solo projects of the backing band through her former fanzine, and has interviewed Bernard, Chuck, Blondie, Tim and Darryl.

Other Fan Meetings with Individual Stones in Private and at Shows

Another one of my respondents has been presented to Keith Richards in private, to her great delight, "an absolutely beautiful experience." Although she worried that she might shake or cry, none of that happened because

> *the man has a gift. He makes it as natural as falling rain. He spent a good long time with me, treated me real special. To have my arms around that precious and beautiful man...*

Keith wanted her arms around him, says the anonymous fan. On other occasions when she'd been within touching distance, people around her said she should touch him. She just thought since he didn't indicate it, he was probably not in the mood for "another pair of hands pawing him." She knew once when he came back to where she was standing, he had recognized "his tribe." Then "when the time came," he did give her the sign that he wanted the touch from her.

The youngest person to meet a Rolling Stone didn't recognize Ronnie when he saw him at a drugstore. Today known as JasontheKeithoholic, the eight-year-old Jason was in line with his mom at a drugstore in 1981 in his hometown of North Brookfield, about a half hour west of Worcester, Massachusetts. Watching a man walking by dressed differently from the males he knew, Jason recalls, "It was the first time I ever saw a man with an earring." Jason went up to Ronnie and asked him about the earring. Patting Jason's head, Ron explained, "It's a fashion statement." As they walked to the car, his mother informed him that he had just encountered one of The Rolling Stones. Shortly after that, Jason got ahold of *Tattoo You* before its official release. He has his own Facebook page listing his homemade CDs called "Keithoholic Records," not outgrowing his Stones love, which his dad termed "a phase he was going through" when he was thirteen, well over two decades ago, as Jason heads toward forty.

A slender woman with defined cheekbones and long hair that changed from dark golden blonde with highlights to medium brunette since I've known her, Little Queenie (LQ) met Charlie once. He came into the Rattlesnake Inn at a show in Oakland on the *Bigger Bang* tour. Her main form of contact is a "rapport" with all of them on the stage since *Licks*, the tour before that. Each one of them will flirt, taking turns with LQ, "and it really comes and goes in waves." On the process, she says

> *they seem to know when they have been playing with me too much and they back off for a while or get subtle, then they break it out again months later.*

The band recognizes her because of frequent attendance and also by how she dances, with flowing, snake-like arm movements, modeled on how some people used to dance at Grateful Dead concerts during their space jams. A fan of theirs, LQ picked up the style though she is too young to have gone to the original Dead shows, first seeing the band in 1985.

Her interactions with Ronnie are probably the most extensive. Once in Austin he yelled at a guard "for about a minute" to give her a guitar pick. He mouthed the words "I love you" from backstage in Chicago. On the other hand, sometimes he is less friendly, as when LQ approached Ronnie to say "hi" in a New York bar. His bodyguard stopped her, telling her Ronnie's wife Jo was there. At her Meet and Greet, the prearranged, pre-show group contact for fans in most cities on *A Bigger Bang* (ABB), Mick crossed the floor to meet with the first group, looked over at her. "I know he recognized me, " says Queenie. When he came over to her group, she was disappointed that he just shook her hand and said "hi" and moved on. She knew his dad had just died. Before that, he had blown kisses and waved and then just the week before Oakland, he sung "She Was Hot" directly to her. He made that intention clear by his expression and when "he walked up to her" twice at the end. She continued her exchanges with band members at a Meet and Greet, an encounter of fans and the band before shows.

Meet and Greets: Groups of Fans Meet the Whole Band

Back at the Meet and Greet in Las Vegas, Keith approached and Little Queenie shook hands with him for a long time, feeling "pretty comfortable with him." Wearing his shades, LQ couldn't see his eyes. He just stood there in front of her. The situation "seemed positive" so she said, "Hey, baby."

> *...he just stood and looked so I repeated it...I couldn't believe I was looking down on him, that he was shorter than me, and I couldn't believe he didn't say anything...*

She felt "his warmth and heart", through the silence. Then it was time for the photo shoot. LQ saw a little space between Keith and Ronnie.

> *I say, "Can I get in between you two?" or something to that effect. They didn't say anything. Keith put his arm around me, but Ron just put his arm on my shoulder.*

Then it was time for them to leave. LQ touched Keith's hand and "we squeezed hands for a second and he was gone." She was talking to the hostess of the meeting, and Charlie came up and "interrupted to say hello!" LQ said "Hello, again." He smiled, looked closely at her, and then walked away. She regretted not telling him they met the week before at the Rattlesnake, not sure if he remembers. She thought he at least recognized her from the shows, because they all watch her dance. She's even caught Charlie watching, before he looks away. At the show a little later, Mick found her dancing in the first song, halfway up at the side of the stage, and pointed at her. Ron looked and then looked away. Keith found her during "Sympathy" and after that, "waved, caught her kiss, and was very attentive" for the next few songs. Charlie looked too.

Queenie says if you weren't there you might think she's crazy. I tell her I understand, from my own experience, not at her level, not nearly as frequent or intense as hers, not meeting Mick, Keith, or Charlie. Other interchanges from the audience between her and Keith continued at the Atlantic City show after Las Vegas. Keith walked up the runway toward her, mouthed "Hey Baby" and she mouthed it back and stuck out her tongue. He reacted with "sounds," which pleased LQ. Another funny thing happened during the no guitar part of "You Can't Always Get What You Want." which was a follow-up to when she was in the onstage seating the year before at Chicago's Soldier's Field. At the show in Stockholm's Cirkus arena, Keith spoke "about eight words" to her and then looked for a reaction. She had no idea what he said, so she just smiled.

Little Queenie attributes her rapport with the band since the *Licks* tour to going to theater shows and her "subsequent ability to get pretty close the stage no matter where." They impress her as generally "very friendly and very flirtatious," running in those "waves" of interaction, peaking and slowing, ebbing and flowing over time.

One of the small number of hardcore fans cast as an extra in the audience for Scorsese's film *Shine a Light*, Moongoddess is an east coast Shidoobee regular. She exudes warmth, and her submitted photo showed enough appeal to make the cut, unlike almost all of the rejected Shidoobees who applied. A blue-eyed brunette, her Mona Lisa smile in a heart-shaped face could charm even the most hardened, most selective casting director, or the most cynical, most curmudgeonly Stones fan. She functions behind the scenes as a co-planner of Shidoobee events, as well as out front, enthusiastically welcoming newcomers in her down-home New Jersey style. She has been to one Meet and Greet with the band at Churchill Downs racetrack in Louisville, Kentucky, and visited the Rattlesnake Inn during the London shows of *A Bigger Bang* tour. Other interactions took place at shows, such as near the front in the Ottawa stadium, where she and three friends stood on chairs in the second row while Keith played directly to them.

Perhaps the biggest thrill for the Moongoddess was meeting the Stones in 2006 at the Churchill Downs racetrack with its "Sacred Hedge," the lush garden near the finish line. The land was also "sacred grounds" for her and "Sweet William" or "Billy," her childhood sweetheart. Married for three years, Billy and Moongoddess reunited to become best buddies fifteen years after their divorce. Her "dear friend and musical soul mate," Billy was killed in the 9/11 disaster. He had worked and lived in Churchill Downs for ten years, the perfect locale for his love of horses, joined with his other passion, the Rolling Stones.

She had gone down to Kentucky, overjoyed to find out at the last minute that her son Evan could come along. That was a dream of hers, to take her 14 year old with her, even though he would have to miss school. When he checked Shidoobee's online list of who was attending, knowing some of the fans from other occasions, Evan decided he could learn more from going to the show than from school. Mother and son were the guests of Stoneman and Mrs. Stoneman who also hosted the "pig gig" event for around 150 Shidoobees and friends on the day after the Louisville show. Stoneman asked guests to check in by placing a pin in their home location on a map of the U.S. and Europe he had created for the party. Fans representing seven states and four countries inserted pins in the map. Moongoddess and Evan stuck their pins in New Jersey.

Adding to the festivities, a resident of the area and a longtime member of Shidoobee, IORR, and Rocks Off, Drake was throwing another party for fans. His post-show party wound up lasting well past the wee hours of the morning, attended by many who were staying overnight for the Stoneman's annual pig gig.

Earlier on the day of the show, after briefly settling in at the Stonemans' house, Moongoddess and Evan heard about the contest at a branch of Radio Shack. The prizewinner would sit on the stage with the band, according to the contest announcement. The local store was a madhouse, according to Moongoddess, with people holding receipts from goods bought at other locations of Radio Shack, making them technically ineligible to qualify for the drawing. The manager held an impromptu Stones trivia contest for the first prize given out, and then called out a number for the second award. Not realizing what the winning prize was, Moongoddess heard her receipt number "876". She wrote on Shidoobee, "When they explained what we had won, I started to tremble and cry....... I was going to meet THE STONES."

Moongoddess continued her description of what happened that evening at the Meet and Greet in detail. She and her son were taken into the venue to partake of a full-course, delicious dinner with accompanying wine that she called "sweet and bitter fruit(s)", quoting the song "Sweet Virginia." Before show time, the two were escorted to the backstage area to become part of the second group of ten fans to prepare to meet the band, a good spot to have, remembers Moongoddess. She learned the rules by watching the first bunch go through the drill: No touching unless one of them touches you first! No cameras or gifts allowed. No rushing at the boys. Mick came bounding out through the curtain before the others, "dancing" into the room. The crowd cheered on seeing them, as she shouted "Shidoobee". All four smiled at that, Ronnie and Keith both wearing their blue Shidoobee bracelets. Moongoddess recounted her feelings on encountering the band in the Meet and Greet space:

> *It is so surreal to experience this..... You are in slow motion but your heart is pounding . YOU feel blessed and honored to be in their presence. They are so personable and down to earth... GREAT eye contact... smiles and lots of hand shaking.*

> *I am pinching myself, IS THIS REALLY HAPPENING? I have never seen Evan smile so widely. We watch as they take a picture with the first group and now MY HEART IS READY TO EXPLODE... I can feel the hair on the back of my neck standing UP.*

It was time for the band to meet with her group, and she would have a turn with each of the boys. As Mick came toward her, so sweet and smiling, "you could feel his energy." When he noticed the tongue tattoo on her cheek, he touched it, and winked. She whispered "Shidoobee". Ronnie approached, "bouncing around" with his big grin. She told him she enjoys his music. Just as he was walking away, she held her arm out to show him her Shidoobee bracelet. He immediately turned, retraced his steps and did a little jig in front of her. "It was freaking great."

When Keith came along, he looked happy and jovial, excited about the upcoming gig happening soon after this gathering with the fans. As they gazed at each other, Moongoddess wondered, "Am I really looking into those eyes?" Keith asked, "Didn't we just meet you?" He recognized her from other shows where he had seen her near the front of the stage. She felt numb, but somehow managed to communicate that she's been following him since 1975 and only now finally gets to really meet him. Keith chuckled and she found herself kissing his cheek. She even asked Evan later if she really did that or if that was just a dream. The last of the four, Charlie came over. After shaking hands and saying hi, she found herself overcome with emotion that Charlie is still with us, after the treatment of his throat cancer. She touched Charlie's face, gently cupping it with both hands, and then kissed his cheek, telling him how glad she is that he is here. She was thinking how blessed we are, recalling her own father, with tears in her eyes.

Moongoddess traced a line back from Churchill Downs to her soul mate Billy, and then to her first meeting Doug and the Shidoobees in Block Island in 2002, enhancing her enjoyment of shows ever after. The line continues forward to this latest "miracle" where she met The Stones face-to-face. She reflected on her experiences, including Keith singing directly to her, Michaelene, Vic and Sharp E from the stage at the Frank Clair Stadium in Ottawa a year before the Meet and Greet, exclaiming, "The Stones know the Moongoddess".

The late, great Art, (Artie) or "RainingBlimps" (RB), told about his Meet and Greet in Las Vegas in November 11, 2006, six weeks after they played in Kentucky. I was lucky enough to interview Artie, a proud alumnus of Ohio University in Athens, Ohio. Known for his humor, he was a very active member of Shidoobee before his untimely passing, posting there daily. A few of his trademark sayings such as his evil laugh, BWAAAAAAAAAAAAAAAAHAHAHHAHAHAHAHAHA!!!" along with his animated Elvis avatar and his signature "HEAR IT FOR A THOUSAND MILES!!!" linked to his profile have made it into other fans' signatures, in memoriam. In Las Vegas, where he resided, he often socialized with a number of Shidoobees passing through his town, arriving there for shows or other purposes.

When Radio Shack in Las Vegas had a contest for a Meet and Greet prior to a show, RB entered through their website every day for 45 days straight, with the help of a pop-up reminder. He put in both his name and his wife Kathy's name. He figured they'd probably want someone local, and sure enough, the winning call came in under her name. She gave her pass to another avid Stones fan, a female friend of theirs. They were both extremely nervous before meeting the whole band. RB had on his Keith Richards Athletic Club T-shirt, honoring his favorite Rolling Stone. When Keith came over to him, he spied the shirt, stepped back to look, and asked RB, "Who's that guy?" Art managed to say, "Gold rings on ya" to him, and Keith repeated it to him in return. RB described the meetings as "quick, one minute...a whirlwind," after the boys all come "busting into the room." Art and his friend knew just where they wanted to be for the shot, and were right near the band at the time. The friend ended up between Mick and Keith in the front, with Artie right behind her, in his cap and black-framed glasses. He cropped the center of the Meet and Greet shot with them between the two Stones to use for his Shidoobee profile.

He had met Ronnie at the art shows in Las Vegas, speaking with him "very briefly." Once Ronnie signed a Shidoobee sticker for him, and he eventually signed the Meet and Greet photo when Artie caught him in town. At one art show in the Jack Gallery at Mandalay Bay, Art was standing at the side near the front door. As Ronnie came in, barging through the crowd, he yelled out, "really loud, 'RONNIE!'

He looked over, reached over his body to shake my hand. He said, "This must be Vegas." It was an automatic reaction. He stuck his hand out.

Along with his Ronnie meetings, he had also met Mick Taylor and Bobby Keys.

Originally from India, Nandita is a petite professor living in Puerto Rico. Through written communications, she campaigned hard to get the boys to play there, and in 1999, her dreams came true. To her shock, Prince Rupert sent her a letter saying, "Thank you for the invitation." Then on a visit to India where they played *Licks* in April 2003, Nandita had the chance to get into a Meet and Greet. An acquaintance managed a hotel and arranged a room for her there, promising he could get her into the Meet and Greet. When she had to cancel her reservation to go to another hotel, Nandita sadly reported, "There went my connection." She got the number of the person "organizing everything" who also had an extra ticket to the show. Nandita dragged her father along, then in his mid-70s. She wanted to go stand in line early, so at first they separated. Her dad

> went wandering off on his own. He ran into this guy organizing the Meet and Greet, and badgered this guy into letting me in. The guy said, "I'll let your daughter in but not you."

There were about ten other people who were given wine and told to wait in an outdoor area. No cameras were allowed, in this year before most cell phones had built-in cameras. To Nandita's excitement, the Stones friended her on Facebook and put up a short video of the occasion. The four came out and shook everyone's hands and gathered for group pictures. Nandita says she "didn't push and shove", that Mick just came and stood next to her. Those she knew didn't believe her story at first, asking her "how many people she had to beat up" to land at Mick's side. The video came out six months later, proving how Mick purposely cut in immediately to Nandita's right, putting his arm around her for the group shot.

My Brief Contact with Band Members at Shows and Elsewhere

My own small brushes with Stones have mainly come from inside the crowds at shows, with the one exception, so far, of meeting one Rolling Stone, Ronnie, in person. I had a pass to attend one of his art shows in Las Vegas, at the Jack Gallery in the Mandalay Bay complex. When I wore the badge to the show that announced I had attended, Ronnie acknowledged me, pointing to the band from the b-stage, which was unexpected and very nice. I had managed to snag a place in the first row there, moving from my seat nearby. Keith played a special riff to me, or so it seemed, making eye contact, and then offering the head, heart and balls sign. I think he had a pick too, but I was too dumb, too unknowing to put out my hand to take it, so he shrugged, put it back, and kept on strumming, going deeper into the music.

The next time I went to see his art, at the same gallery, Ronnie was running even later than usual. I was standing at some distance from the gallery doors, but within sight, out in front in the hallway of Mandalay Place. All of a sudden, Ronnie strode in, and nodding to the guys with him, he walked up to me alone as I was saying "Hi". He said, "Hi" back, put out his hand to shake, and added, "Thanks for coming!" Totally charmed and nonplussed that this famous guy would thank me, just like I was coming to his weekend luncheon, I croaked out "Thank *you*" and he thanked me again. I stood motionless for a time. Since I had already seen the exhibit earlier when the doors first opened, I decided to leave. That night Ronnie was mobbed, surrounded and blocked by the pushing crowd inside to the point that he panicked, understandably. He soon isolated himself in a back room and stayed there for the next hour or two, only speaking to fans who had bought his paintings that night, one to one, in private.

My interactions with Mick have likewise taken place at shows, with again, one exception, though I was still part of a crowd. As I waited outside the Beacon Theatre across the street where the New York police insisted we stand before the performance in honor of Bill Clinton's sixtieth birthday, the principal players arrived, one at a time. Keith had brushed by me and another Shidoobee when we walked close to the stage door entrance before we were told to vacate the space, kicked out, first to the curb, and then over to the other side of the street. L'Wren came by at one point, and I shouted hello to her. She turned and waved at me. When Mick emerged from his car, he took time to stand and wave to the crowd. I couldn't see him very well, so I walked from my original spot toward the right over to the far left of the fifty or so fans standing there. He found me on that side, making eye contact and gesturing, as if asking, "What the heck are you doing?" moving his head back and forth like he was looking for me. I laughed and felt gratified. I guess I shouldn't have been so surprised that he recognized me, with my big straw Stones cowboy hat, black with a red tongue on the front. I went to quite a few shows on that tour.

Before *A Bigger Bang*, I had seats occasionally close enough to interact with Mick, most notably once in Columbus, with a fifth row aisle ticket bought from eBay, back when people would sell online for face or less. When he sounded the first notes on his harmonica for "Can't You Hear Me Knocking," I let out a scream of joy. He looked at me sternly, as if to say wait, let me get into this, I'm concentrating. Minutes later, he stared straight at me, head on, doing his swaying dance moves during a quieter instrumental break. Another time in Las Vegas, I was one of the only people standing up in my section of the audience, and Mick and Ronnie started waving at me. I'm did a double take, thinking who are they looking at? They then pointed at me, saying, you, you, you, and we were all laughing. Then, playing around, Mick hit Ronnie with some kind of prop, a yellow rubber bat, I think, like he used to do when Ronnie was still drinking.

In London, during the last three shows of ABB, Mick saw me once on the floor, standing up on a metal folding chair, as the rolling B-stage was going back to the main stage. I blew him a kiss, and he returned it, looking at me. This time it is Mick who does the double take, widening his eyes in surprise, acting like what are you doing in Europe? We laughed. I loved it. The ushers made me and the mostly much younger females get down off the chairs soon after that. We had crashed the area for a closer look at the B-stage. The next night Mick saw me in the second row next to the stage on the side, and came right up. He performed at length to me, for me, for maybe ten seconds, waving his arms to the music, and staring into my eyes. My new UK pal Flairville from IORR, was wildly dancing to the left of me. Witnessing this, he stopped, looked from Mick to me, and said, "Wow." Great moments in time, oh, yeah.

When I started going to shows, I would not have conceived of the Stones making such personal contact, even though I knew it happens between a musician onstage and attentive fans in the audience. They are musicians and performers, at base, no matter how big the crowd. I mean, it's only rock 'n roll, but I like it.

EPILOGUE:

DON'T STOP: STONES' FUTURE, FANS' FUTURE

"Each show is such a treasure and such a gift." (NeverBreak)

As I write this epilogue, this conclusion, the *14 on Fire* Tour has ended in Europe, with a pause until the makeup dates in Australia and New Zealand, eight of those completed in November, 2014. Dates for South and Central America were first solidifying for spring, and then possibly in doubt until fall, 2015. Fans await a brief return to the U.S. including a rumored appearance at the "Rock in Rio" fest in Las Vegas in May 2015, along with a few more cities in the States, and then possibly somewhere in the UK to end the current run.

Whatever is in the future for The Stones, this recent round of shows from 2012 through 2014 has shown the band is far from finished. Only a downturn in their continued desire to keep doing what they've worked at nearly all their lives, or a decline the health of one or more of the four core members would stop them from performing.

This volume may add a perspective to the reams of pages written about The Rolling Stones. Some of what the fans think from the start up to the near present about the appeal of the band and some of what they feel when they hear the music comes through here in these pages.

Fans will still have the three public boards, Shidoobee, IORR, and Rocks Off and private lists, such as the private email Undercover, and other sites for the band and for individual band members. They have their recorded music, and most of all, their memories from live shows.

At Shidoobee, the talk is primarily about where they will play in the States. At IORR, it's centered around London, as they haven't played there since 2012. Others claim MSG in NYC is "their real home," protested by those who note their national origins in the UK. They've played in Brooklyn next to Manhattan and Newark, NJ, close by. Fans debate which group of shows were better, the series in 2012 and 2013 in the U. S. or the shows in Europe in 2012, 2013, and 2014, along with the 2014 shows in Asia and Abu Dhabi. Those from Europe generally pick shows there, having seen more of them. With most of the shows coming later to Europe, the band was more practiced that time around. On the other hand, in the U.S, for a few shows, Mick Taylor participated in two songs, rather than only one, "Midnight Rambler," and at one show in California he was onstage for three. These featured spots for their former guitarist don't count in "Satisfaction," where Mick T typically played acoustic guitar. The band played indoor venues in the States and added "the pit" for audiences there, and wherever they could elsewhere. The last group of shows in Australia and New Zealand played to very responsive crowds with the band perhaps at its best level yet in this period.

The *50 and Counting* 2012 shows in the UK and almost all of those in the States in 2013 included a guest artist for one song per show, usually not someone loved by a Stones crowd, some doing better than others. While the novelty of guests seemed to inspire the band at times, the vocalists trading off with Mick, the fan reaction was lukewarm to many of them, especially toward musicians not known to fit with The Stones' style. Fans appreciated that these guests replaced the traditional warm-up band, skipped over by many fans in previous tours. In contrast, guests such as John Mayer might stop by in 2014 to perform an opening set in Rome. There were guest spots during some shows in Europe's *14 on Fire* as in the U.S. and the British shows in 2012, including Bruce Springsteen, Gary C. Clark, and the local singer Tomoyasu Hotei in Japan.

All rehearsed with the band before that night's show, but some had prepared better than others. On *50 and Counting*, Gwen Stefani exhibited little familiarity with her tune, from what I heard, and Taylor Swift pirouetted better than she sang, for example. Boos from the crowd jolted Mick Jagger for a moment, at the start of his duet with Ms. Swift. Unless you were a fan of Lady Gaga, her number didn't work for much of the crowd, from where I stood. On the west coast, Bonnie Raitt, a sometime opener for the band, and John Fogerty did okay. Springsteen at least had an irresistible energy and enthusiasm that sparked a charge in the crowd. I saw Katy Perry up close and came away impressed with her poise on her song. She didn't even blink when Mick flipped her hair up with his hand during "Beast of Burden." Aaron Neville pulled out "Under the Boardwalk," covered by the Stones early on, a nice surprise for fans at the second Philly show. Eric Clapton and Jeff Beck, who had played with band members before, and whose fans overlapped with The Stones worked somewhat better in England during *50 and Counting*. From her band Florence and the Machine, Florence and Mick danced very well together, in an impromptu routine. He kept signaling for her to turn away from him to face the crowd. She preferred to stay sideways, inches from his face, for much of the number. In my view, she was one of the better guest artists to perform, in a recurring attempt to replace Lisa Fischer's solo spot on "Gimme Shelter," before Lisa returned to sing it.

Most people came away from these last tours with renewed respect for the band, enjoying their playing. A notably different tone permeated the interactions between Mick and Keith on the last tour in 2014. Feelings between the childhood friends, observed from the stage, and in interviews with each man, had chilled over the years, to a virtually frozen state on *50 and Counting*. For the film *Shine a Light* filmed during *A Bigger Bang*, viewers wondered how hard Mary Scorsese had to press the two to share a microphone on "Far Away Eyes." Before the 2012 shows, Keith admitted that he felt compelled to apologize to Mick for a few remarks about Mick that appeared to widespread coverage in his autobiography *Life*, published in October 2010. At several points during shows on *14 on Fire*, they sang close together, Mick with his hand mic and Keith using the standing mic. Keith had his arm around Mick's shoulders. They often encountered each other and interacted in harmony onstage or on the ramps face-to-face, different from the avoidance most overtly displayed by Mick on earlier tours.

Ronnie's ongoing sobriety and newfound happiness with his third wife Sally Humphries led to joyous and consistent playing during the last two tours. Keith's recovery from his brain hemorrhage and surgery after a fall during *A Bigger Bang* seemed to improve his concentration and playing. Perhaps another factor in the renewed vigor of performance from the band as a whole is Mick losing his companion of nearly 13 years, L'Wren Scott, who committed suicide near the start of the last tour in March 2014. The band postponed the Australian/New Zealand segment of the tour, apparently banding together in Mick's grief over L'Wren's death. Reading in from afar, I surmise that Mick could count on Keith, Ronnie, and Charlie to carry out his wishes to take a break, and then pick up the tour again with rehearsals for Europe, after the Far East shows. Such support in a crisis seemed to affect the unity of the band. Another fan brought up how Mick's mood and demeanor may well be brightened by the noticeably increased level of Keith's and Ronnie's playing and probable dependability onstage since *ABB*.

Also for the last two tours, a few of the auxiliary musicians were cut: Blondie Chaplin on vocals and guitar and horn players Kent Smith and Michael Davis. These changes are heralded by those who prefer a stripped-down band: Longtime backup player Tim Ries and an added Matt Clifford supplemented Chuck Leavell on keyboards at times, also playing their primary instruments of saxophone and French horn. Lisa Fischer and Bernard Fowler sang back-up on shows from 2013 onward, and Bobby Keys played his sax with Tim on select tunes.

Only the band knows what really lies ahead. They predicted only a few years for themselves at the start. Mick has often said that people have thought they were done since 1969. Fans who count on live shows went through the draught of the 80's, were satisfied in the 90's and held their breath through the later years during gaps in tours. This last run from late 2012, set up to continue until late in 2014 and into 2015 was almost unexpected, given the uncertainty of them playing together for a while. But--it's what they do, since their late teens and early twenties. Since the start of *50 and Counting*, they have performed in limited runs, rather than announcing massive world tours. They appear to want to test the waters, to see how the shows go, first with the shows in London and the New York/New Jersey areas in November and December. If the band is satisfied, and the fans are there, they go ahead with each phase, making sure to take breaks for at least two days, if not three, between shows.

Fans have easily accessible outlets online, much more active during tours, of course. Together they can reminisce, even when the last run is over, which they do already, about past shows and recordings, and relationships among band members. How long they will continue to do this will depend upon the board leaders' willingness to keep their fan groups running. If these boards have anything to do with the band's legacy, people will continue talking about the band collectively and publicly for a very long time. The band has passed its music and performances to their own and their fans' children and grandchildren, who will continue liking them and discussing them individually well into the future, past my own lifetime. Their influence on rock musicians, and thus, fans of many other bands that came after them is virtually indisputable.

Noted podcaster Marc Maron in *Attempting Normal* (2013, p. 71) writes about remarkable musicians: "That's what your heroes can do for you -- lift you vicariously above the dirty work of life and conjure a different way of being."

Thank you Rolling Stones.

ACKNOWLEDGEMENTS

Here I want to thank the people who helped me most in making this book possible. First, here are those who did interviews with me, without whom the book would not exist:

3dteafoe, Aidan, akissaway, Anon, Arthur/Michael, astearsgoby, BaboonBro, Beast, Bernie, blindmellon, BlueLena, Buckeyedave,, Calista,, candyfromstrangers, CarlTheLobsterman,

cherryohbaby, Chicago_Dave, CindyC, crisscrossmind, deardoctortake1, delilah, detroitgirl, diane d, DPOY, drake, durtysox, eastcoaststeve, EG Jim/EG Tom, edith groves, elmo lewis, exiledinmedina, fareastbam, fenwayjoe, flairville, Fred Hardin,

Gaby, GAFF. gazza, gin, glencar, hbwriter, HonkyTonkWom99, inopeng, IRLTS, jaggerfan1, jaggerlover, jagken, jasonthekeithoholic, JDel, joe chavez, Jumping_Jack, JChavez925, kmrc4ever, lademore, Lance, little queenie, lovelyladyjane, mattlee, michael from Germany, michelejagger, Mickijaggeroo, mirajagga, MiJim, moondog, moongoddess, MRDEEEEE, muncy, Nandita, oldkr, partydollmeg, Paulina, phillyrob, Philippe Puicouyoul, Promo, rainbow, RainingBlimps, ripper,

Rockman, Rod35, Saintofme, Schoolboyblues, Steve Portigal, stikkyfingers, stones75, stonesbreath, Stonesdoug, stonesmarie, stonesriff1, Stoneszone9, SullenMorbius,

Sully, sweetcharmedlife, TheMakuleGuy, timbernardis, Thru and Thru, Tina, TomL,

tydyelady, UrbanSteel, Voodoo Chile in Wonderland, voodoopug, Yesterdayspapers, ugotthetsilver.

These are more kind folks, including fans who provided information at crucial times, and others who aided my efforts:

Amber, anon, Baron Wolman, benstones, Betz, Bill German, brownsugar5,Cindy Jagger, crossfire hurrcane, Dan O'Reilly, Darth Bowie/Michael DeStefano, Deb White, Diane L, drbryant, ellip, GimmeLilDrink, gostonesg, Greg Martin, Helen Killoran, igtba, ijwthstd , jason in NM, Joanne, Johnny Otiac, Jon Plotkin, Joseph, joyce in NM, Kay Jeffrey, keno, Marilou Regan, naomi, naturalust/tod page, nursejane, Patrick Drumm, Paul, Priscilla Long, Rachel Spring, Stillafool, stonedinTX, txgrl, VirginiaJagger, Wembley, winter.

To my editor and publisher, Nell Minow, your support and assistance are invaluable.

To everyone who provided pictures of themselves, a thousand thanks.

The photo of Glenn and Mick is by Glenn Schneider. Used with permission.

About the Author

 Dr. Andrea J. Baker (aka andee or angee) talked to fans from online communities for **You Get What You Need: Stories of Fans of The Rolling Stones,** a book for anyone who likes rock music or has followed a band.   Andee is a sociologist who has written about online communities, relationships, identities, communications online, and social movements.

Cover designed by Scarlett Rugers Book Design Agency
www.booksat.scarlettrugers.com

Graphic on front cover by artist Kristen Thiele

Author photo by andee

Miniver Press publishes lively and informative non-fiction books about history, music, movies, sports, business, politics, and culture. For more information, see http://www.miniverpress.com

Made in the USA
Columbia, SC
10 June 2019